영어 1등급을 위한

ENGLISH READING COMPREHENSION & LITERACY

결국은 문해력

주제 。요지편 제1권

이성태

결국은 문해력 제 1 권 주제 요지편

발   행 | 2024 년 1 월 25 일
저   자 | 이성태
펴낸이 | 한건희
펴낸곳 | 주식회사 부크크
출판사등록 | 2014.07.15.(제 2014-16 호)
주   소 | 서울특별시 금천구 가산디지털 1 로 119 SK 트윈타워 A 동 305 호
전   화 | 1670-8316
이메일 | info@bookk.co.kr

ISBN | 979-11-410-6883-7

www.bookk.co.kr
ⓒ 이성태 2024

_____

저 자

이성태
현, TED 영어 원장
현, 육군 3 사관학교 토익강사
토익 만점 강사
수능,토익,토플,텝스 17 년 강의 경력
북미(미국,캐나다) 6 년 거주
University of British Columbia ESL
경북대 대학원 영문학 석사
경북대 대학원 영문학 박사과정

Preface 서문

집필 취지

수능영어뿐만 아니라 텝스, 토플, 토익, 등 영어시험은 각기 다른 목적을 가지고 있지만, 공통적으로 중요시되는 것은 바로 "독해력"과 "문해력"입니다. 특히, 수능에서의 영어 독해문제는 단순히 언어의 이해나 문장의 해석을 넘어서, 다양한 전문분야의 학술적이고 관념적인 글을 이해하고 분석하고 추론하는 능력을 요구합니다. "결국은 문해력" 시리즈는 이러한 수능영어의 특성을 고려하여 학생들이 영어독해의 본질을 파악하고, 체계적이고 논리적인 독해 훈련을 통해 영어실력을 향상시키는데 기여하리라 확신합니다.

최근 수능영어의 경향

최근 3년 간(22-24학년도) 기출 지문의 출처를 분석해 보면, 영어권의 대학 학부생뿐만 아니라 대학원생을 대상으로 출판한 학술 서적이나 논문 등에서 발췌된 지문들이 상당히 많습니다. 영미권 최고 대학교 중 아래 7개 대학출판사(Harvard, Oxford, Cambridge, Yale, MIT, Stanford, Princeton)에서 출간된 학술서적에서만 최근 3년간 수능 독해 지문 중 13개 이상의 지문이 그대로 발췌되어 출제되었습니다. 그리고 학술서적을 전문으로 하는 유명한 'Routledge' 출판사에서 발행된 학술서적에만 23-24학년도 수능에서 5개의 지문이 출제되었습니다. 그 외 유명한 대형 출판사들의 대학교재나 전문서적 등에서 발췌되었습니다.

한국의 수능 영어 출제자들은 직접 지문을 만들거나 원서 지문을 수정하지 않고 그대로 사용합니다 (실용문과 듣기 제외). 그리고 다양한 분야의 학술지나 논문에서 한 문단만을 발췌해서 수능문제로 만들기 때문에 발췌된 글들은 상당히 학술적이고 관념적인 내용이 많아 한글 해석본을 봐도 아주 난해한 경우가 많습니다. 소위 말하는 킬러 문항은 미국 현지 대학생들에게 조차도 어려워 풀지 못합니다. 필자가 2015년부터 2020년까지 미국에 거주하면서 현지 학생들에게 매년 수능영어 문제(킬러 문항)중 몇 문항을 풀어보게 했습니다. 대부분 학생들은 고개를 절레절레 흔들며 한국 고등학생들이 영어를 진짜 잘하나 보다라고 말하기도 했습니다. 이렇듯 수능영어는 일상 영어를 넘어 논리적 사고력과 추론능력을 요구하고 있습니다.

특히, 최근 수능영어에서 빈칸 추론, 글 순서 정하기, 한 문장 삽입 등의 문제는 상당히 난해해서 기존의 단순한 요령이나 비법?으로는 문제해결이 되지 않습니다. 문장 해석위주의 구문/유형 독해의 기존 학습법의 한계를 넘어서야 합니다. 문장과 문장과의 관계와 영어의 글 전개구조를 파악하는 훈련과 논리적 사고를 통한 추론능력을 키울 수 있는 체계적인 훈련과 연습이 절대적으로 필요합니다.

교재의 목표와 기대

"결국은 문해력" 시리즈의 '제1권 주제·요지편'은 단순히 문장 해석을 넘어서 문장과 문장과의 논리적 전개와 한글과 다른 영어의 글 전개 구조를 이해하도록 도와줄 것입니다. 그리고 독해의 핵심 능력인 주제와 요지 그리고 뒷받침 글을 파악하고 암시된 요지를 추론하는데 필요한 논리적인 사고를 향상시키는 데에 중점을 두고 있습니다.

결국은 문해력" 시리즈는 총7권으로 구성될 예정입니다. 본 교재는 필자가 십 몇 년 전에 집필한 영어 독해 교재 3권(*Basic Reading Skills, Essential Reading Skills, Critical Reading Skills*)을 기반으로 최근 수능 경향에 맞추어 수정 보완해서 나오게 되었습니다. 향후 출시될 "결국은 문해력" 시리즈는 *제2권 핵심과 뒷받침 글 구별하기, 제3권 글 전개방식 익히기, 제4권 글 순서와 문장 삽입, 제5권 요약과 패러프레이징, 제6권 추론하기, 제7권 Fact와 Opinion* 등입니다. 각 권마다 영어 독해력과 문해력을 높이기 위한 다양한 전략과 실전 연습이 계속해서 제시되며 수업생들의 영어 실력이 한 단계씩 발전되기를 기대합니다.

저자

Table of Contents

Chapter 1

Topic & Main Idea

What you need to learn:

1

Plato (c. 428-347 B.C.)

❝One of the penalties for refusing to participate in politics is that you end up being governed by your inferiors.❞

— **Plato** (428–347 B.C.), ancient Greek philosopher

❍ 플라톤이 한 이 말은 무엇에 관한 것인가? _____

1.1. What is a Topic?

Topic 이란?

> ### "What is this about? What is the general idea?"
>
> 의미를 이해하기 위해 글을 읽을 때는 반드시 글의 Topic을 찾는 것부터 시작해야 한다. Topic을 파악하면 지금 읽고 있는 글의 내용과 이미 알고 있는 지식을 쉽게 연결할 수 있다. Topic을 찾기 위해서 자신에게 이렇게 질문해보자:
>
> ### "무엇에 관한 내용이지? 포괄적인(general) 내용은 무엇이지?

Example

다음 각각의 그룹에 있는 단어들 중에 한 단어가 나머지 다른 모든 단어들을 포함하는 Topic이 된다. 아래 각 항목에 포괄적 내용인 Topic을 찾아 동그라미 표시를 하라.

1. jealousy시기,질투   hatred증오   (emotion감정)   worry걱정,근심   pride자부심,긍지

2. spiders   cockroaches   mosquitoes   insects   ants

3. chemistry   science   physics   biology   genetics

4. penny   nickel   dime   quarter   coin

5. robbery   murder   kidnapping   assault   crime

 Explanations

1. emotions   2. insects   3. science   4. coin   5. crime

각 항목의 Topic은 그 외 다른 단어들의 의미를 포함하고 있으며 그 외 모든 단어들은 Topic에 대한 구체적인 예들이다.

PRACTICE 1

아래 각 항목에서 항목별로 다른 모든 단어들의 **Topic**이 되는 한 단어를 찾아 동그라미 표시를 하시오.

1. square   circle   triangle   (shape)   diamond   sphere

2. kneeling   position   standing   sitting   reclining

3. air bags   seat belts   car equipment   spare tire   rear-view mirror windshield   wipers   anti-lock brakes

4. encyclopedia   dictionary   reference book   atlas telephone directory

5. Mercury   Venus   Earth   Mars   Jupiter   Saturn   Neptune Planet

6. cough   sneeze   symptom   sore throat   rash   headache runny nose

7. Won   Yen   Dollar   Pound   Currency   Euro   Yuan

8. literature   poetry   novel   drama   play   critique

9. household chores   sweeping   mopping   dusting   vacuuming washing   folding   ironing   tidying

10. climate change   deforestation water scarcity   biodiversity loss overfishing   environmental issues   habitat destruction pollution

PRACTICE 2

아래 각 항목의 단어들을 포괄하는 Topic을 쓰고 그 Topic에 적합한 항목 한 가지를
빈칸에 쓰시오.

Ex. Quebec   Toronto   Montreal   Ottawa   <u>Vancouver</u>

     Topic: <u>Canadian cities</u>

1. snowy   humid   rainy   stormy   breezy   sticky   _____

   Topic: _____

2. mountains   plateaus   plains   cliffs   valleys   basin   _____

   Topic: _____

3. greed   cowardice   selfishness   dishonesty   cheating   _____

   Topic: _____

4. reliability   determination   responsibility   honesty   _____

   Topic: _____

5. freezing   cold   cool   lukewarm   scorching   _____

   Topic: _____

6. fiction   non-fiction   mystery   fantasy   biography   poetry   _____

   Topic: _____

7. dawn   sunrise   noon   sunset   dusk   midnight   _____

   Topic: _____

Thanks! **Explanations**

1. Weather Conditions: overcast흐린 mild온화한 muggy후덥지근한
2. Geographic Features: hills   ravine협곡
3. Negative Traits/ Characteristics: betrayal배신 deceit사기,기만
4. Positive Characteristics: generosity관대함 integrity진실성;고결함;성실 sincerity진정성 dependability신뢰성
5. Temperature Intensities강도: blazing타는 듯한 burning
6. Literary Genres: drama
7. Times of the Day: twilight황혼,땅거미

PRACTICE 3

다음 단어와 어구들은 어떤 글의 세부적인 내용(Specific Ideas)들이다. 이 글의 **Topic**을 예상해 보고 가장 적절한 항목에 동그라미 표시를 하시오.

1. *Specific Ideas:*

count to ten, take a deep breath, go for a walk

Topic: a. actions

       b. ways to calm down

       c. ways to calm down just before a test

2. *Specific Ideas:*

eat out less often,   rent movies instead of going to the theater,   buy clothes on sale,   use coupons at the supermarket

Topic: a. ways to save money

       b. ways to waste money

       c. ways to enjoy life

3. *Specific Ideas:*

rainforests,   important,   many reasons,   carbon dioxide into oxygen, fight pollution,   sustain the Earth,   purify water,   provide food

Topic: a. purified water in rainforest

       b. importance of rainforest

       c. rainforests on the Earth

4. *Specific Ideas*:

middle ages,   simple sundials,   14th century,   regulation difficulties,
spring-powered clocks,   accurate mechanical clocks,   public clocks,
improved accuracy,   digital clocks,   smart watches

Topic: a. accuracy of clocks

b. various clocks

c. development of clocks

5. *Specific Ideas:*

putting sticky tape on someone's chair,   putting a "kick me" sign on
someone's back,   putting hot pepper in someone's cereal

Topic: a. jokes

b. practical jokes

c. practical jokes played on teachers

PRACTICE 4

다음 어구들은 어떤 글의 세부적인 내용(Specific Ideas)들이다. 주어진 세부 내용들을 읽고 글의 Topic으로 가장 적절한 것을 고르시오.

1. *Specific Ideas:*

- create a cozy reading nook at home

- utilize audiobooks during long commutes

- join a book club to discuss favorite reads

- build a personal reading challenge for the year

cozy 아늑한 **utilize** 활용하다 **commute** (회사)통근 **enhance** 강화하다 **alternative** 대안의;대안

Topic: a. ways to enhance reading habits

b. alternative reading formats

c. benefits of reading communities

2. *Specific Ideas:*

- avoiding bottled water and using a reusable bottle

- repairing and repurposing old items instead of discarding them

- taking advantage of cashback and discount apps

- learning basic car maintenance to avoid costly repairs

reusable 재사용가능한 **repurpose** ~에 다른 목적(용도)를 갖게 하다
discard 버리다 **take advantage of** ~을 이용하다 **maintenance** 유지 관리, 보수 **costly** 값비싼

Topic: a. ways to save money

b. ways to save our environment

c. ways to keep our communities clean

3. *Specific Ideas:*

- decline in TV cable subscriptions
- Netflix and Amazon Prime Video in the streaming market
- impacting the way people consume entertainment
- algorithms to analyze user preferences and provide personalized recommendations

subscription 구독 impact ~에 영향을 끼치다 consume 소비하다 analyze 분석하다 preference 선호

Topic: a. impact of online streaming services

b. history of online streaming services

c. benefits of online streaming services

4. *Specific Ideas:*

- Easy access to drugs can increase the likelihood of experimentation.
- Adolescents may succumb to peer pressure to fit in with a certain social group.
- Teenagers are often curious and may experiment with drugs to explore altered states of consciousness.
- Media portrayal of drug use can influence teenagers' perceptions and make drug use seem more socially acceptable or glamorous.

access to ~ 에 접근, ~에 대한 이용 likelihood 가능성 experimentation 실험 adolescent 청소년
succumb to ~에 굴복하다 fit in with ~와 어울리다 altered state 변화된 상태 consciousness 의식
portrayal 묘사 perception 지각, 인식 glamorous 매력적인 get addicted to ~에 중독되다

Topic: a. reasons why adolescents take drugs

b. factors why teenagers get addicted to drugs

c. how teenagers get easy access to drugs

1.2. What is a Paragraph?

문단이란 무엇인가?

아래 문단처럼 보이는 두 글이 있다. 두 글에 속한 문장들을 주의 깊게 읽어 본다. 두 글은 모두 문단(Paragraph)이라고 말할 수 있는가?

Group A

In the world of pets, there are many types of animals that people keep as companions. Some people have dogs, and others have cats. Fish are also popular pets. People like pets because they are cute and provide companionship. Dogs can be trained to do tricks, and cats like to cuddle. Fish require a tank and need to be fed regularly. Taking care of their pets costs a lot, and giving them food, water, and attention is also demanding. Overall, having a pet can bring joy and happiness to a person's life.

Is this a paragraph?　Yes / No

Group B

Pets play a significant role in enhancing the emotional well-being of individuals. The companionship of a dog or cat provides comfort and reduces feelings of loneliness. The act of petting an animal releases oxytocin, the "bonding hormone," promoting a sense of connection and happiness. Studies have shown that interacting with pets can lower stress levels and improve overall mood. Whether it's a playful kitten or a loyal canine companion, the positive impact of pets on human life is a source of joy and comfort.

Is this a paragraph?　Yes / No

What is the difference between Group A and Group B?

Group A: 이 단락은 <u>하나의 Topic에 대해 일관성 있게 글을 전개하고 있지 않</u>다. 도입부에는 '다양한 유형의 반려동물의 종류와 일반적인 정보'를 나열하고 후반부에는 '애완동물을 돌보는 일은 비용이 많이 들고 힘든 일'이라는 문제를 제기한다. 그리고 아무런 근거를 제시하지 않고 마지막 문장에서는 '전반적으로 애완동물은 개인의 삶에 기쁨과 행복을 줄 수 있다'고 글을 맺는다. 이 글은 하나의 Topic에 대한 일관성 있는 글이 아니므로 문단이 아니다.

Group B: 모든 문장들이 <u>반려동물이 인간의 정서적 건강(emotional well-being)에 미치는 영향</u>이라는 특정한 하나의 Topic에 대해 통일성을 가지고 일관되게 글을 전개하고 있기 때문에 효과적인 좋은 문단이다.

문단의 정의는 다음과 같다. 영어로 된 정의 문장을 소리 내어 읽고 외우세요.

Definition of a Paragraph

> **A paragraph is a group of sentences developing one single topic.**
>
> 문단의 모든 문장들은 하나의 **Topic**에 관해 통일성 있게 전개되어야 한다. 그러므로 문단에는 반드시 하나의 **Topic**이 있어야만 한다.

수능영어는 문단으로 시작해서 문단으로 끝나는 시험이다. 문단의 제목, 주제, 요지, 필자주장, 요약, 빈칸 추론, 글 순서, 한 문장 삽입, 그리고 흐름상 어색한 문장 찾기 등 모든 문제가 한 문단에 관한 것이고 이 모든 문제가 한 문단으로만 이루어져 있다. 그래서 문단의 정의에 대한 명확한 이해가 수능영어 문제 해결의 시작이다.

PRACTICE 1

다음 문장들의 그룹이 문단인 것과 문단이 아닌 것이 있다. 주의 깊게 읽고 문단인지 아닌지를 구별하고 문단이면 Topic을 적으시오.

Group 1

People are happy with developments in medicine. Then they worry about the increased number of births. Scientists make great advances in agricultural chemistry, greatly increasing our food supply. Then our rivers become so polluted that we cannot even swim in them. We are happy with the developments in air transportation and impressed by the great airplanes. Then we are frightened by the horrors of air crash or air war. We are excited by the fact that space can now be entered. But we will undoubtedly see the other side there, too. [수능]

Is this a paragraph?   Yes or No

If yes, what is the topic?   _____

Explanations

이 글은 좋은 문단이다. 문단의 주제는 "기술 진보의 이중성(Dualities of Technological Progress)"이다. 이 글은 기술 진보에 대한 인간 반응의 양면성(ambivalence of human reactions to technological progress)을 제시하며, 초기의 기쁨과 낙관주의를 묘사하고 의학, 농업, 항공 운송 및 우주 탐사의 발전과 관련된 우려와 부정적인 결과를 설명한다. 즉, 모든 문장들이 기술 진보의 양면성과 의도하지 않은 결과라는 하나의 주제로 상호 연결되어 있다. 그러므로 이 글은 응집력 있고 통일성 있는 좋은 문단이다.

[어휘] **agricultural chemistry** 농 화학 **polluted** 오염된 **air transportation** 항공 운송 **air crash** 비행기 추락 **space** 우주 **undoubtedly** 의심할 여지없이 **the other** 나머지 하나(의)

Group 2

For fewer tourists, lower prices, and more beautiful scenery, head for the Sagres Peninsula. The regional museum has a rich collection of costumes, weapons, and handicrafts. Buses will get you to most places, but for long trips, trains are cheaper and more comfortable. The Portuguese economy has expanded very rapidly in recent years, but it still has many problems. In the 15th century, Lisbon was a worldwide center of political power, religion, and culture.

Is this a paragraph?   Yes or No

If yes, what is the topic?   _____

Explanations

이 글은 일관성이 부족하고 하나의 Topic에 대한 명확한 초점이 없기 때문에 문단이 아니다. 문장들은 여행 조언, 교통 정보, 포르투갈 경제의 현재 상태, 15세기 리스본에 대한 역사적 세부 사항 등 관련 없는 다양한 주제들을 나열했을 뿐이다.

[어휘] **scenery** 경치, 풍경 **head for** ~로 향하다 **peninsula** 반도 **collection** 소장, 모음집 **costume** 복장, 의상 **handicraft** 수공예품 **expand** 팽창하다 **rapidly** 급속하게 **religion** 종교

Group 3

In the world of video gaming, character customization has become an integral feature that enhances player engagement. Players can personalize the appearance, skills, and abilities of their in-game avatars, creating a unique gaming experience. Whether choosing hairstyles, outfits, or specialized skills, character customization allows players to express their individuality and immerse themselves in the virtual world. This feature has become a popular aspect of role-playing games, where the journey of the player's character is shaped by their decisions and preferences.

Is this a paragraph? Yes or No

If yes, what is the topic? _____

 **Explanations**

이 글은 비디오 게임과 캐릭터 커스터마이징(Video gaming and character customization)이라는 특정 주제에 대해 논의하는 문단이다. 캐릭터 커스터마이징의 목적, 기능 및 역할-놀이 게임에서의 인기에 대한 세부 정보를 제공한다.

[어휘] customization 커스터마이징, (고객,사용자) 맞춤화, 주문형 integral feature 필수적인 기능(특징) enhance 강화(향상)시키다 engagement 참여, 몰입도; 약혼 personalize 개인화(개별화)하다 outfit (겉)옷, 복장, 차림새 individuality 개성 immerse oneself in ~에 몰입하다 aspect 측면 preference 선호(도)

Group 4

The development of Artificial Intelligence has been rapid. We see AI in various forms, from voice-activated assistants to self-driving cars. AI can analyze vast amounts of data quickly, helping in fields like healthcare and finance. However, there are ethical concerns about how AI is used. Some worry about privacy issues and the potential misuse of AI. Others argue that AI will open new avenues for job creation, demanding a workforce equipped with skills in data analysis, machine learning, and AI development. Automation and AI can also lead to job displacement as machines become capable of performing tasks that were previously done by humans. So, it's crucial to address these ethical concerns as we embrace the advancements in AI technology.

Is this a paragraph? Yes or No

If yes, what is the topic? _____

Thanks! Explanations

인공 지능의 신속한 발전과 다양한 응용 분야 소개를 한 후 윤리적 문제를 제기한다. 그런데 다음 문장에서 어떤 사람들은 잠재적인 취업 창출에 대한 긍정적 측면을 주장한다고 말한다. 논리적으로 맞지 않는 전개이다. 그리고 나서 뜬금없이 자동화와 AI가 직업 이직을 초래한다는 부정적 측면을 강조한다. 그리고 마지막 문장에서는 윤리적 우려에 대한 해결이 중요하다고 말한다. 전혀 일관성과 논리가 맞지 않는 글이다. 그래서 이 글은 AI의 여러 중요한 측면들을 소개하지만 특정한 Topic에 대해 일관성 있게 글이 전개되고 있지 않기 때문에 좋은 문단이 아니다. 잘 구성된 문단은 중심 아이디어나 주제를 중심으로 일관성 있게 글을 전개해야 한다.

[어휘] **voice-activated assistant** 음성 인식 비서 **self-driving car** 자율 주행 자동차 **analyze** 분석하다 **finance** 금융 **ethical** 윤리적인 **potential misuse** 잠재적 오용 **open new avenues for** ~을 위한 새로운 길(장)을 열어주다 **workforce** 인력 **equipped with** ~로 장비를 갖춘, ~을 겸비한 **job displacement** 직업 이직(대체) **become capable of ~ing** ~할 수 있다 **crucial** 중대한, 중요한 **address** 해결하다 **embrace** 포용(수용)하다 **advancement** 진보, 발전

1.3. Topic of a Paragraph

 문단의 **Topic** 찾기

여러분이 문단을 읽을 때는 **"이 문단은 무엇에 관한 것이지?"**라고 항상 자문해야 한다. 즉, 문단 안의 모든 문장들이 동일하게 언급하는 대상이 무엇인지 생각하면서 글을 읽어야 한다. 이러한 과정을 통해 문단의 Topic을 파악하게 된다. 그리고 Topic은 "너무 광범위한(too broad)" 것이 되어서도 안 되고 "너무 좁은(too narrow)" 것이 되어서도 안 된다.

Example A: What is this paragraph about?

People who are addicted to shopping have a high need for excitement and a low self-esteem. There seem to be two types of addicted shoppers. One is the daily shopper, who cannot miss a single day at the stores. The other is the binge buyer, who goes shopping weekly to buy huge numbers of things.

be addicted to ~에 중독이다 **addict** 중독자 **self-esteem** 자존감

이 문단의 **Topic**으로 가장 적절한 것을 고르시오. 그리고 문단의 **Topic**에는 **T**자를, "너무 광범위한(too broad)"것에는 **B**자를, "너무 좁은(too narrow)"것에는 **N**자로 표시하라.

_____ Addicts

_____ Shopping addicts

_____ The binge buyer

 Explanations

이 문단의 Topic은 "쇼핑 중독자"이다. "중독자"는 모든 종류의 중독자를 포함하기 때문에 너무 광범위하다. "The binge buyer"는 너무 좁은 것이다.

Example B: What is this paragraph about?

The cost of printing money and then destroying old ones has become too expensive for the government. As a result, considerable efforts are being taken to replace the dollar bill with a dollar coin. The dollar coin will last far longer than a dollar bill. It could also be used in vending machines easier than a dollar bill. Additionally, this change could benefit cities as they spend a lot of time counting dollar bills placed in collection boxes, which a dollar coin could solve.

considerable (수, 양) 상당한 replace A with B A를 B로 교체하다
last 지속되다 vending machine 자판기 benefit ~에게 이익(혜택)을 주다 collection box 수거함

이 문단의 Topic으로 가장 적절한 것을 고르시오. 그리고 문단의 Topic에는 **T**자를, "너무 광범위한(too broad)"것에는 **B**자를, "너무 좁은(too narrow)"것에는 **N**자로 표시하라.

_____ Using a dollar coin in a vending machine

_____ Reasons for adopting a dollar coin

_____ A dollar coin

 Explanations

이 문단의 Topic으로 "Reasons for adopting a dollar coin" (달러 동전을 채택하는 이유들)이 가장 적절하다. 대부분의 문장은 달러 동전이 달러 지폐보다 낫다는 이유를 제시한다. Topic으로 "Using a dollar coin in a vending machine"는 '너무 좁은' 의미이고 "A dollar coin"은 '너무 광범위한' 의미이다.

PRACTICE 1

각 문단의 **Topic**으로 가장 적절한 것을 고르시오. 그리고 문단의 **Topic**에는 **T**자를, "너무 광범위한(too broad)"것에는 **B**자를, "너무 좁은(too narrow)"것에는 **N**자로 표시하라.

1.

If you smoke, your blood may be harmful to other people's health. According to one study, the blood donated by smokers contains high levels of pollutants that stay in the blood for up to thirty days. Someone receiving that blood may be deprived of oxygen and thus need another transfusion.

pollutant 오염물질 be deprived of ~을 박탈당하다 oxygen 산소 transfusion 수혈

_____ The dangers of smokers' blood

_____ The dangers of smoking

_____ How long pollutants stay in smokers' blood

2.

Graffiti can be seen in many places, ranging from bathrooms to skyscrapers. Can you guess who is more likely to be responsible for them, men or women? It turns out that both men and women must share the blame for graffiti. A recent study found that females produce most of the graffiti on bathroom walls. In contrast, males are responsible for most of the graffiti on outdoor walls.

range A from B (범위가) A에서부터 B까지이다 skyscraper 고층빌딩 It turns out that S+V~ ~인 것으로 판명되다

_____ Environmental problems

_____ Bathroom graffiti-makers

_____ Makers of graffiti

3.

Phobias are fears that are out of proportion to the actual dangers in given situations. For example, some people have a phobia about elevators. They worry that if they enter an elevator, the cable will break and they will fall hundreds of feet to their death. While such an accident can happen, it is extremely rare. Another instance of a phobia is a fear of medical needles. Some people will refuse to receive an injection, even if they are seriously ill. They fear the pain of the needle or the possibility that it might not be sterile, even in the doctor's office.

be out of proportion to ~ 와 비례하지 않다 rare 드문, 희귀한 injection 주사, 주입 sterile 무균의, 소독된; 불임의

_____ Fears

_____ Phobias

_____ Phobias about elevators

4.

Would you take an airplane trip sitting in the thirteenth row of seats? Go to a doctor on the thirteenth floor of the medical center? Of all superstitions, few are as widely believed as the one saying the number thirteen is unlucky. So many people are uncomfortable with thirteen that the number is eliminated from most airline seating charts. Many high-rise apartments and office buildings have a twelfth floor and a fourteenth floor─ but nothing in between. In France, houses are never numbered thirteen. And the national lottery in Italy doesn't use the number.

---

superstition 미신 **eliminate** 제거하다, 없애다 **number** ~에 번호를 매기다

_____ The superstition about the number thirteen.

_____ Buildings without a thirteenth floor

_____ Superstitions

5.

For centuries people believed that sleep-walkers were possessed by evil spirits. These spirits forced them to wander throughout the night. Researchers today say that other, more worldly causes are behind sleepwalking. First of all, nighttime wandering may result from stresses and frustrations built up during the day. Also, the tendency to sleepwalk can be inherited. This was illustrated by the report of a patient at a California sleep disorder clinic. He once woke up in the dining room during a family reunion and found himself surrounded by sleepwalking relatives.

sleep-walker 몽유병 환자 be possessed by ~에 사로잡혀 있다 evil spirit 악령 worldly 세상의, 세속적인, 물질적인 be inherited 유전되다 illustrate 설명하다, 묘사하다 disorder 장애 relatives 친척

_____ Sleep

_____ Causes of sleepwalking

_____ The inherited tendency to sleepwalk

6.

Although people dream of being celebrities, the disadvantages of fame are great. First, the famous must look perfect all the time. There's always someone ready to photograph a celebrity looking dumpy in old clothes. The famous also give up their privacy. Their divorces and other problems end up on the evening news and in headlines. Even worse, celebrities are often in danger. They get threatening letters and are sometimes attacked.

celebrity 유명인사(the famous) **dumpy: short and fat**   **end up** ~ (결국)~하게 되다 **threatening letter** 협박 편지

_____ The privacy of celebrities

_____ The dark sides of fame

_____ The dangers of fame

7.

People who don't brush their teeth regularly usually have bad breath. While inadequate oral care is a common cause of bad breath, other factors can contribute as well. A throat infection is one source of bad breath. Even excessive consumption of coffee or alcohol can cause bad breath. And a stomach problem resulting in acid buildup can be a contributor, as well.

---

inadequate 부적절한 oral care 구강 관리 bad breath 입 냄새, 구취 contribute 원인이 되다; 기여하다 contributor 원인; 기여자 infection 감염 excessive 과도한, 지나친 consumption 소비 acid buildup 위산 축적

_____ Bad breath

_____ Causes of bad breath

_____ Bad breath caused by oral and throat infection

Brush Your Teeth!

8.

A growing number of people are expected to know how to use computers to satisfy the demands of their job. Without proper training, workers are prone to injuries of the hand, wrist, and back. Working at the computer demands proper angles. The top of the monitor should be at eye level, so that the center of the screen is viewed slightly downward. The keyboard should be on a flat surface, with one's arms relaxed, loose, and at a ninety-degree angle. Forearms and hands should be parallel to the floor. The back should be angled slightly to the rear to increase blood circulation and reduce compression of the spine. The chair should fit the curve of the lower back, with the seat angling forward slightly to reduce pressure on the spine.

be prone to ~받기(입기) 쉽다

forearm 팔 뚝 **be parallel to** ~와 평행이다 **circulation** 순환 **compression** 압박, 압력 **spine** 척추

_____ Computers on the job

_____ Tips for using a computer on the job

_____ Injuries caused by using a computer on the job

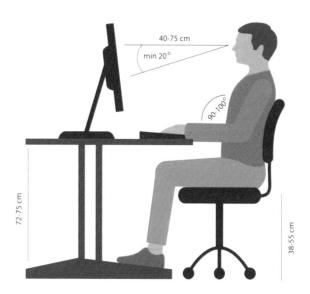

1.4. What is the Main Idea

Understanding the Main Idea

요지 이해하기

가장 중요한 독해기술은 필자의 요지(Main Idea)를 찾는 것이다. 요지는 포괄적인 내용(General Idea)으로 한 문단의 중심 생각(Central Pont)을 말해 준다. 즉, 문단의 **요지는 Topic에 대한 필자의 생각**으로 종종 문단에서 한 문장으로 나타나는데 이 문장을 **주제문(Topic Sentence)** 혹은 **요지문(Main Idea Sentence)**이라 한다. 문단의 그 나머지는 요지를 뒷받침해주고 설명해주는 세부적이고 구체적인 내용의 문장들(Supporting Sentences)로 이루어져 있다.

The Main Idea as an "Umbrella" Idea

글의 요지를 "우산"개념으로 생각해보자. 이 "우산"은 문단의 모든 세부사항을 다 포함하고 있다. 요지는 필자의 주장이며, 나머지 부분은 요지를 뒷받침하는 세부사항으로 예시, 이유, 사실, 그리고 다른 증거들로 이루어져 있다.

Companies have various ways of offering lower prices.

One way of doing this is a trade discount.

Also, a cash discount is a lower price offered to people who pay in cash.

Finding the Topic Sentence

주제문 찾기

★주제문을 찾는 절차 방법

글의 요지(Main Idea)를 찾기 위해서는 다음과 같은 **2** 가지의 질문을 자신에게 해야 한다. 그리고 이 질문에 대한 답을 찾으려고 생각하면서 글을 읽어야 한다.

> *1st Q*: 이 글은 <u>무엇에 관한 내용이지?</u> ➜ 먼저 **Topic**을 찾아라!
>
> 일단 Topic을 찾았으면 빨리 글을 읽으면서 2 번째 질문을 자신에게 하라!
>
> *2nd Q*: **Topic**에 대해 필자가 말하고자 하는 바가 뭐지?
>
> ➜ 그 답이 "**Main Idea**" (요지)이다. 필자는 종종 이 요지를 한 문장으로 나타낸다. 이 문장을 "**Topic Sentence**" (주제문)이라 한다.

Example A: 아래 문단을 읽고 물음에 답하시오.

[1]Americans love to send greeting cards. [2]For instance, over 4 million birthday cards are sent out in this country every day. [3]During Valentine's Day last year, over 900 million cards were mailed. [4]And close to 3 billion holiday greeting cards were sent out over the Christmas season.

1. What is the *topic* of the paragraph? _____

2. What is the *topic sentence* of the paragraph? _____

 Explanations

Topic: Greeting cards

Topic sentence: Americans love to send greeting cards.

Supporting details:

1. 4 million birthday cards are sent out every day.
2. 900 million cards on Valentine's Day were mailed.
3. 3 billion cards over the Christmas season were sent out.

* Sentence 1: 첫 문장이 가장 포괄적 내용(General Idea)으로 문단 전체 내용을 포함하고 있으며 요지를 나타내는 Topic Sentence이다.

PRACTICE 1

아래 문단을 읽고 문단의 Topic 과 Topic Sentence을 찾으시오.

1.

¹Garbage disposal is an enormous problem in the United States. ²We must deal with over a billion pounds of garbage every day. ³That number is equal to about six to seven pounds of solid waste per person. ⁴A large amount of garbage is burned, but that creates air pollution. ⁵Ravines and swampy areas have been used for garbage, but such dumping locations near cities are fast being used up.

---

enormous 거대한, 엄청난 solid waste 고형 폐기물 ravine 협곡 swampy 습지 be used up 소진되다

---

1. What is the *topic* of the paragraph? _____

2. What is the *topic sentence* of the paragraph? _____

 Explanations

Topic: Garbage disposal

Topic sentence: Garbage disposal is an enormous problem in the United States.

Supporting details:

1. We must get rid of a billion pounds every day: six or seven pounds per person.
2. Burning garbage creates air pollution.
3. Dumping locations are being used up.

2.

¹For their own benefit, companies have various ways of offering lower prices. ²One way of doing this is a trade discount. ³It is offered to the shops or businesses that buy goods on a large scale and sell them. ⁴There is also a quantity discount, which is offered to individuals who order large quantities of a product. ⁵The company gives a price break to these buyers because they help cut the costs of selling, storing, shipping, and billing. ⁶Finally, a cash discount is a lower price offered to people who pay in cash.[수능변형]

---

trade discount 거래 할인 **price break** 가격 혜택(우대조치) **shipping** 배송 **billing** (요금)청구

1. What is the *topic* of the paragraph? _____

2. What is the *topic sentence* of the paragraph? _____

Explanations

Topic: Types of Discount Pricing

Topic sentence: For their own benefit, companies have various ways of offering lower prices.

Supporting details:

1. One way of doing this is a trade discount.

2. There is also a quantity discount, which is offered to individuals who order large quantities of a product.

3. Finally, a cash discount is a lower price offered to people who pay in cash.

3.

[1]Will cyber schools replace traditional schools some day? [2]In spite of their problems, traditional classrooms hold many advantages over online classes. [3]First of all, traditional classrooms are a place where students may relate to one another face to face. [4]That is, a keyboard will never be able to replace the warmth of a handshake, or a monitor the smile of another student. [5]In traditional schools, students may also take part in team sports, club activities, and school festivals – choices not available to students who learn through computers. [수능변형]

---

replace 대체하다, 교체하다 **in spite of** = despite ~ 임에도 불구하고 **take part in** ~에 참가하다

1. *The topic is*

   a. benefits of online classes

   b. demand for online classes

   c. advantages of traditional classes

2. *The main idea is stated in sentence _____.*

4.

[1]Whether ruffled or ridged, potato chips got their start because of a hard-to-please restaurant customer in 1853. [2]In that year, George Crum was working as a chef at an elegant resort in Saratoga Springs, New York. [3]He prepared thick-cut French-fried potatoes for diners there. [4]But one diner kept sending his potatoes back to the kitchen, complaining that they were too thick for his taste. [5]Crum cut the potatoes thinner and thinner and finally, very annoyed, made a serving of potatoes too thin and crisp to eat with a fork. [6]To his surprise, the guest loved them. [7]Other guests demanded a taste. [8]Soon "Saratoga Chips" were the most popular item on the menu.

ruffled or ridged 주름진 혹은 융기 된
hard-to-please 기쁘게 하기 힘든 **elegant** 우아한 **a serving of** ~(음식)의 1인분 **crisp** 바삭한

1. *The topic is*

 a. ruffled potato chips

 b. origin of potato chips

 c. potato chips

2. *The main idea is stated in sentence _____.*

1.5. Identifying Topic, Main Idea, Supporting Details

Topic, 요지, 뒷받침 글 구별하기

글의 요지(Main Idea)를 빨리 파악하기 위해서는 **Topic**과 **요지** 그리고 요지를 **뒷받침하는** 세부사항들(Supporting Details)을 구별하는 연습이 필요하다. 세부사항들은 이유, 예시, 부연설명, 연구 및 실험결과, 통계자료 또는 사실적 증거들로 글의 요지를 뒷받침해주는 역할을 한다.

요지를 뒷받침하는 세부사항과 그렇지 않는 부분을 분명하게 구별할 줄 아는 것은 논리적 독해력과 비판적 사고에 매우 중요하다. 특히 수능영어에서 흐름상 무관한 문장 찾기, 문장 순서 정하기와 한 문장 삽입, 그리고 빈칸 추론 문제 해결에 많은 도움이 된다.

아래 네 개의 항목은 각각 하나의 Topic과 하나의 Main Idea 그리고 두 개의 Supporting Details로 구성되어 있다. 각 항목을 읽고 항목 앞에 다음과 같이 표시하시오.

> **T** – for the topic.
> **MI** – for the main idea
> **SD** – for the supporting details

Example A: 각 항목 앞의 빈칸에 T, MI, SD 중 해당되는 하나를 표시하시오.

_____ a. Countless children have learned letters and numbers from *Sesame Street*.

_____ b. For thirty years, *Sesame Street* has taught American children a great deal.

_____ c. *Sesame Street*, the children's TV show.

_____ d. The show has also covered such important topics as love, marriage, and death.

Explanations

이글의 Topic은 '*Sesame Street*, the children's TV show'이고, 이 Topic에 대해 필자가 말하고자 하는 요지는 a. '셀 수 없이 많은 아이들이 *Sesame Street*에서 글자와 숫자를 배웠다.' 이다. 그리고 나머지 두 항목은 요지를 뒷받침하는 Supporting Details이다.

PRACTICE 2

아래 네 개의 항목은 각각 하나의 Topic과 Main Idea 그리고 두 개의 Supporting Details로 구성 되어있다. 각 항목을 읽고 항목 앞에 다음과 같이 표시하시오.

> **T** – for the topic.
>
> **MI** – for the main idea
>
> **SD** – for the supporting details

Group 1

_____ a. The human skeleton has certain important functions.

_____ b. The skeleton gives the body support and shape.

_____ c. The skeleton protects internal organs.

_____ d. The human skeleton

skeleton 해골 support 지지, 지탱 internal organs 내부 장기

Group 2

_____a. TV has begun to deal with sex in a more realistic way.

_____b. Couples on TV now openly discuss topics such as birth control.

_____c. Bedroom scenes are now being shown in detail on some TV shows.

_____d. TV's treatment of sex

deal with ~을 다루다, 취급하다 realistic 사실적인 birth control 피임 treatment 취급

* *Hint: Each item is about how television handles sex.*

33

Group 3

_____ a. One pitcher smooths the dirt on the pitcher's mound before he throws each pitch.

_____ b. One infielder sits in the same spot on the dugout bench during every game.

_____ c. Some baseball players think that certain superstitious habits help them win games.

_____ d. Baseball players

pitcher 투수 smooth ~을 매끄럽게 하다
dirt 흙 throw pitch (공)을 던지다, 투구하다 infielder 내야수 superstitious 미신의

Group 4

_____ a. At dinnertime, instead of cooking many people simply go to a fast-food restaurant, or they send out for pizza or Chinese food.

_____ b. More and more families bring home prepared meals from the frozen-foods section of the "deli" counter.

_____ c. Home cooking is becoming a lost art.

_____ d. Home cooking

frozen-foods section 냉동 음식 코너 a lost art 잃어버린 예술(기술)

Group 5

_____ a. Benjamin Franklin discovered that lightning is an electrical charge.

_____ b. In addition to being a statesman, Franklin was a scientist and an inventor.

_____ c. Benjamin Franklin's work

_____ d. Franklin invented bifocals, the Franklin stove, and an electric storage battery.

---

electrical charge 전하 **in addition to** ~ 이외에, ~에 더하여 **stateman** 정치인
bifocal 이중 초점 렌즈; 원시·근시 양용 안경 **electric storage battery** 전기 축전지

Group 6

_____ a. Scientists used to think of the brain as the center of an electrical communication system.

_____ b. The way scientists view the brain's role has changed greatly.

_____ c. Today it is known that "the brain is a bag of hormones," as one scientist puts it.

_____ d. How scientists think about the role of the brain

---

used to V ~ 하곤 했다 **think of A as B** A를 B로 생각하다 **as + S + puts it** 말하는 것처럼

Group 7

_____ a. Adults seek out spicy or bitter foods to stimulate their smaller supply of taste buds.

_____ b. Sensitivity to flavors

_____ c. The difference in the sensitivity to flavors between children and adults lies in the taste buds, the tiny taste receptors that line the tongue.

_____ d. Young children's tongues are loaded with taste buds and are especially sensitive; therefore, sour or spicy flavors seem too intense to them.

seek out 추구하다, 찾다 **stimulate** 자극하다 **taste buds** (혀의) 미뢰, 미각(능력)
sensitivity to flavor 맛에 대한 민감성(예민함) **receptor** 수용체, 수용[감각] 기관
line 안감을 대다, ~을 감싸다 **be loaded with** ~로 가득 차 있다(싣고 있다) **intense** 강한, 강렬한

Group 8

_____ a. Procrastination has two possible causes.

_____ b. Many people may procrastinate because they have a fear of failure, and if they don't begin a task or project, they can't fail at it.

_____ c. Causes of procrastination

_____ d. Others may procrastinate out of laziness; these careless workers have not yet developed a strong work ethic.

procrastination (일을)미루는 것 **procrastinate** 미루다 **out of laniness** 게으름 때문에 **work ethic** 직업 윤리

Group 9

_____ a. A snake can control its body temperature in two ways.

_____ b. First, a snake can darken its skin to absorb higher levels of solar heat; once its body reaches a suitable temperature, the snake can lighten its skin color.

_____ c. A snake also spreads and flattens its body as it lies at a right angle to the sun's rays to expose more of its body and raise its temperature; to reduce its body temperature, a snake lies parallel to the sun's rays or moves into the shade.

_____ d. Ways a snake controls its body temperature

–Adapted from Smith & Smith, *Elements of Ecology*, 4th ed., p.11

darken ~을 어둡게하다 once+S+V ~ 일단 ~하면
lighten ~을 밝게하다 flatten 평평하게 하다, 펴다 expose 노출시키다 parallel to ~와 평행하게

PRACTICE 3

아래 다섯 개의 항목은 각각 하나의 Topic과 Main Idea 그리고 세 개의 Supporting Details로 구성 되어있다. 각 항목을 읽고 항목 앞에 다음과 같이 표시하시오.

T – for the topic.
MI – for the main idea
SD – for the supporting details

Group 1

_____ a. The Covid-19 pandemic significantly affected education worldwide, bringing about new and difficult changes.

_____ b. The impact of the Covid-19 pandemic on education.

_____ c. Remote learning technologies have become essential tools in the face of pandemic-related closures.

_____ d. The pandemic also made it clear that not all students had equal access to technology and the internet, which made it harder for some to keep learning.

_____ e. The pandemic prompted educators to innovate, adopting virtual classrooms, online assessments, and collaborative platforms.

---

pandemic 전염병 bring about ~을 초래하다 remote learning 원격 학습 in the face of ~에 직면하여 closure 폐쇄 make it clear that S+V~ 을 분명히 하다 access to ~에 대한 이용,~에 접근, 접속 promote 촉진시키다, 증진하다 innovate 혁신하다 adopt 채택하다 assessment 평가 collaborative 협업의, 공동의

Group 2

_____ a. Disagreeing parties can accept the status quo, agreeing to just live with the situation as it stands.

_____ b. When faced with a disagreement, the parties involved have several ways to proceed.

_____ c. One party may use physical, social, or economic force to impose a solution on the others.

_____ d. Negotiation, or reaching a mutually acceptable solution, is a means of dealing with conflict.

_____ e. Various ways for the parties to proceed in case of disagreement.

---

disagreeing parties 동의하지 않는 당사자들 **status quo** 현 상황, 현상 유지 **as it stands** 현재 상태 그대로 **be faced with** ~에 직면하다 **disagreement** 불일치, 의견 충돌 **parties involved** 관련 당사자들 **proceed** 나아가다, 진행하다 **impose** 강요하다, 부가하다 **negotiation** 협상 **mutually** 상호, 서로 **means** 수단, 방법 **deal with** ~을 다루다 **conflict** 갈등, 분쟁

Group 3

_____ a. Algorithms play a significant role in curating and recommending online content.

_____ b. By analyzing user preferences, behavior, and data, algorithms can personalize the online experience by suggesting articles, videos, and ads that are likely to be of interest to individuals.

_____ c. There are concerns about the potential biases and echo chambers that algorithms may create, as they can reinforce existing beliefs and limit exposure to diverse perspectives.

_____ d. Algorithms are employed to filter user-generated content on platforms, removing content that violates community guidelines to maintain a safe and respectful online environment.

_____ e. The role of algorithms in shaping online content.

curate 기획하다 preference 선호도 personalize 개인화하다 article (신문, 잡지) 기사 potential bias 잠재적 편견 echo chamber 반향실(효과) reinforce 강화하다 existing belief 기존 신념 exposure 노출 diverse 다양한 perspective 관점 be employed 적용(사용)되다 filter 거르다, 여과하다 user-generated content 사용자 생성 콘텐츠 respectful 존중하는

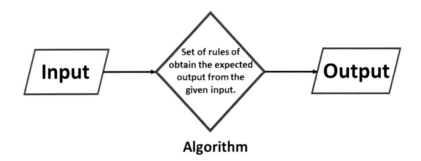

Algorithm

Echo Chamber Effect 반향실 효과

반향실 효과(Echo Chamber)는 뉴스 미디어 정보를 이용하는 이용자의 기존 신념이 닫힌 체계로 구성된 커뮤니케이션에 의해 증폭, 강화되고 같은 입장을 지닌 정보만을 지속적으로 되풀이 수용하는 현상을 비유적으로 나타낸 말이다. "반향실"에 들어선 사람들은 자신이 지닌 기존의 관점을 강화하는 정보를 반복해서 습득되어 이로 인해 부지불식 간에 확증 편향(Confirmation Bias)을 가지게 될 수 있다. 반향실 효과는 사회적이나 정치적인 의견이 극단화(Extremism)되는 현상을 증가시키며 극단주의의 배경이 되기도 한다. 반향실은 원래 소리의 잔향 효과를 위해 설치된 공간을 뜻하는 것으로 미디어 비평에 비유적으로 사용된다.

Group 4

_____ a. K-pop music groups like BTS and BLACKPINK have gained immense popularity, breaking records and topping charts not only in South Korea but also internationally.

_____ b. Korean dramas, known for their unique storytelling and high production quality, have attracted a global audience, leading to remakes and adaptations in various countries.

_____ c. The Korean Wave, also known as Hallyu, has made a significant impact on popular culture worldwide.

_____ d. The influence of Korean fashion and beauty trends can be seen in the global market, with K-beauty products gaining popularity and Korean fashion brands becoming sought-after worldwide.

_____ e. The global impact of the Korean Wave

immense 거대한, 엄청난 **top charts** 차트 1 위를 차지하다
adaptation 각색, 개작; 적응 **trend** 경향, 추세, 유행 **sought-after** 수요가 많은, 인기 있는

Training 적용 훈련 문제

아래 각 문단을 읽고 주제문(Topic Sentence)을 찾고 아래 질문에 답하시오.
반드시 주제문을 찾는 절차 방법 2단계 지침을 따르면서 빨리 독해 할려고 노력하라!

1.

¹The number of animal species categorized as endangered or threatened is on the rise. ²In 1985, there were 329 species listed by the U.S. Fish and Wildlife Service as being endangered or threatened. ³This year, there are 402 species listed. ⁴In addition, there are over 3,000 other species that experts have not yet examined, some of which may also meet the criteria for inclusion on the list.

endangered or threatened (동,식물) 멸종 위기에 처한
on the rise 증가하고 있는(increasing) **meet** 충족시키다(satisify) **criteria** 기준 **inclusion** 포함

1) 주제문의 위치? _____

2) 글의 주제로 가장 적절한 것을 고르시오.

    a. criteria for listing species as endangered or threatened

    b. increase in the number of endangered and threatened species

    c. role of the U.S. Fish and Wildlife Service in species conservation

2.

[1]There are many actions that individuals should take to care for their pets. [2]But the opposite is also true — numerous studies have shown that owning a pet can improve a person's mental and physical well-being. [3]A pet that a person feels attached to improves the owner's frame of mind. [4]A pet gives a feeling of being needed to the person who takes care of it. [5]Pets also give an unconditional love that makes coming home after a rotten day more bearable. [6]Even being in the same room as a pet can lower one's blood pressure and heart rate.

feel attached to ~에 애착을 느끼다 **unconditional** 조건없는 **rotten** 불쾌한, 좋지않은; 썩은 **bearable** 견딜 수 있는, 참을 만한

1) 주제문의 위치? _____

2) 글의 주제로 가장 적절한 것을 고르시오.

   a. actions individuals should take to care for their pets

   b. studies on the impact of pet ownership on well-being

   c. importance of mental and physical well-being

3.

[1]Zoos used to be places where unhappy-looking animals paced back and forth in tiny cages. [2]But nowadays, many zoos have large "natural" habitats in which animals can live as if they were in the wild. [3]In some zoos, for instance, chimpanzees and gorillas live in large areas that look like rain forests. [4]Huge animals such as elephants wander freely on "African plains" in the heart of New York City and San Diego. [5]Zookeepers occasionally use such environments to encourage animals to work for their food, as in the wild. [6]In one zoo, for example, honey is hidden in a fake anthill. [7]Chimpanzees scoop the honey out with a stiff piece of hay, which is the process similar to how they "fish" for insects in Africa.

used to +V~ 하곤했다 **pace back and forth** 이리저리(앞뒤로) 왔다갔다하다
habitat 서식지 **plain** 평원 **anthill** 개미집 **scoop out** (국자 등으로) 퍼내다 **stiff** 뻣뻣한

1) 주제문의 위치? _____

2) 글의 주제로 가장 적절한 것을 고르시오.

   a. history of zoos and their evolution

   b. living conditions of animals in zoos

   c. role of zookeepers in animal care

4.

[1]Photo radar is increasing the efficiency of ticket giving. [2]With photo radar, a beam is directed at oncoming traffic. [3]When a speeder is detected, a picture of the front of the vehicle is taken. [4]The license number is matched with the car's owner, and a ticket is sent. [5]The arresting officer does not have to take time explaining the situation to one motorist while others speed by. [6]Also, the load on traffic courts is lessened since people are sent a copy of the picture that was taken. [7]Photo radar has shown itself to be a practical and effective means of enforcing speed limits.

---

efficiency 능률, 효율성 **ticket giving** 티켓 발부 **be directed at** ~로 향하다 **license number** (차량) 면허 번호 **be matched with** ~와 일치하다 **arresting officer** 체포 경찰관 **load on traffic court** 교통 법원에 대한 업무량(부하) **be lessened** 줄어들다 **show itself to V** ~ 인것으로 입증되다 **practical** 실용적인 **effective** 효과적인 **enforce** 시행하다

---

1) 주제문 2 개의 위치는? _____

2) 글의 주제로 가장 적절한 것을 고르시오.

   a. efficiency of photo radar in traffic law enforcement

   b. how photo radar works to catch speeding drivers

   c. advantages of using photo radar in issuing tickets

   d. reducing the burden on traffic courts with photo radar

Challenge  1등급 도전

다음 글을 읽고 주어진 질문에 답하시오.

1.

Although aspirin has been available in drugstores for only a century, it's been in use for thousands of years. About 2,400 years ago, the physician Hippocrates prescribed willow bark, which contains a natural form of aspirin. It wasn't until the early nineteenth century, however, that chemists created a simpler version of that ingredient. Unfortunately, though, it ate the lining of the stomach. In the late 1880s, a chemist named Felix Hoffmann conducted further experiments, and he created an effective fever and pain medication with fewer side effects. In January 1899, the German company Bayer trademarked the name "Aspirin" for this new drug, which was made available to those with a doctor's prescription. Today, Americans alone take 12.5 billion aspirin tablets, gelcaps, and caplets a year.

---

1. *What is the topic of the paragraph?*

    a. natural forms of aspirin   b. history of aspirin   c. Hippocrates

2. 아래 빈칸에 'use' 동사를 사용하여 요지문을 완성하시오. (동사형태 변형 필요)

    Main Idea: Aspirin _____ _____ _____ for thousands of years.

 Explanations

[정답] 1. b, 2. <u>has been used</u>

[해석]

비록 아스피린이 단지 100년 동안 약국에서 사용되었지만, 그것은 수천 년 동안 사용되었다. 약 2,400년 전, 의사 Hippocrates는 자연적인 형태의 아스피린인 버드나무 껍질을 처방했다. 그러나 19세기 초에 화학자들이 그 성분의 더 단순한 버전을 만들었다. 그러나 불행하게도, 그것은 위 벽을 손상시켰다. 그러나 1880년대 후반, Felix Hoffmann이라는 화학자가 더 많은 실험을 해서 부작용이 적은 효과적인 해열과 진통제를 만들었다. 1899년 1월, 독일 회사 Bayer가 이 신약의 이름을 "Aspirin"으로 등록상표 했으며, 의사의 처방을 받은 사람들에게 제공되었다. 오늘날, 미국인들만 1년에 125억 개의 아스피린 알약, 젤 캡, 그리고 캐플렛을 먹는다.

[해설]

이글의 요지는 "Aspirin <u>has been used</u> for thousands of years." (아스피린은 수천년 동안 사용되었다)이다.

[어휘]

physician 의사 **prescribe** (약을) 처방하다 **prescription** 처방(전) **willow bark** 버드나무 껍질 **It is not until A that S+V~.** A 해서야 비로소 ~하다 **chemist** 화학자 **ingredient** (구성) 성분 **lining of the stomach** 위벽 **conduct** (실험 등을) 수행하다 **fever and pain medication** 해열 진통제 **side effect** 부작용 **trademark** ~을 등록상표 하다 **tablet** 알약

2.

Can intelligence be taught? The traditional answer is no. That answer, however, is based solely on short-term studies. Long-term studies have shown that training in specific skills does seem to improve intelligence scores. For example, the Israeli psychologist Reuven Feuerstein has developed a program that involves hundreds of hours of special tutoring. The program's emphasis is on remedying errors in thinking. Feuerstein's results suggest that such training does indeed improve IQ scores. A program in Venezuela has produced similar results.

---

1. *What is the topic of the paragraph?*

    a. intelligence tests   b. improving intelligence   c. Reuven Feuerstein

2. 빈칸에 주어진 단어를 사용하여 요지문을 완성하시오. (동사형태 변형 필요)

    Main Idea: Long-term research suggests that _____

    can _____.

                           (intelligence/ training/ improve/ be/ with/scores)

 *Explanations*

[정답] 1. B 2. <u>Intelligence scores</u> can <u>be improved with training.</u>

[해석]

지능을 가르칠 수 있는가? 전통적인 답은 아니다. 그러나 그것은 단기적인 연구에 기반한 것이다. 장기간의 연구들에 따르면, 특정한 기술훈련이 지능 점수를 향상시키는 것처럼 보인다고 한다. 예를 들어, 이스라엘의 심리학자인 Feuerstein은 수백 시간의 특별한 과외를 포함하는 프로그램을 개발했다. 프로그램의 강조점은 사고의 오류를 고치는데 있다. 그의 Feuerstein의 결과에 따르면 그러한 훈련이 정말로 IQ 점수를 향상시킨다는 것을 암시한다. 베네수엘라에서의 한 프로그램도 비슷한 결과를 낳았다.

[해설]

이 글의 요지는 "Long-term research suggests that <u>intelligence scores</u> can <u>be improved with training.</u>"(장기간의 연구에 따르면, 지능 점수는 훈련을 통해 향상될 수 있다)이다.

[어휘]

intelligence 지능 **be based solely on ~** 전적으로 ~에 근거를 두다(기반한 것이다) **emphasis** 강조 **remedy** ~을 치료하다; 치료(법) **suggest** (연구 결과가) 나타내다, 암시하다

3.

When an animal is injured, the first thing it will do, if it possibly can, is scramble to its feet. Despite the fact that doing so will probably cause further pain, the instinct to get up drives the animal because the alternative, taking no action to get up, invites predators to come in to kill and eat the defenseless one. Emotionally, we do the same thing. Often a person who has just suffered an injury or a devastating shock or loss will answer, "Fine" when asked, "How are you doing?" Just labeling this as denial misses the deeper truth. The organism, animal or human, is trying not only to look fine in order to _____, but trying to be fine. This is resilience in action.

— Adapted from Marian K Volkman, *Life Skills: Improve the Quality of Your Life with Applied Metapsychology*, 2nd ed. 2022, p.26

*scramble to one's feet: 재빨리 일어나다 **resilience** 회복 탄력성

1. 빈칸에 들어갈 말로 가장 적절한 것은?

    a. avoid attack

    b. gain support

    c. make profits

    d. draw attention

    e. suppress anger

2. 이 글의 주제로 가장 적절한 것은?

    a. physical and emotional resilience of animals and humans in the face of threats

    b. common survival strategies between animal and human behavior

    c. instinctual responses to injury: the drive to avoid predators

    d. denial as a protective mechanism: coping with pain and injury

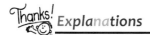

Explanations

[해석]

어떤 동물이 다쳤을 때, 그것이 어떻게든 할 수 있다면 가장 먼저 할 일은 재빨리 일어나는 것이다. 그렇게 하면 더 심한 통증을 유발한다는 사실에도 불구하고 일어나려는 본능이 그 동물을 몰아붙이는데, 그 이유는 일어나려는 동작을 전혀 취하지 않는 다른 방법이 포식동물이 다가와 방어력을 상실한 동물을 죽여 먹게 하는 결과를 초래하기 때문이다. 정서적인 면에서 우리들도 똑같은 반응을 보인다. 이제 막 부상 또는 참담한 충격이나 상실을 당한 사람은 흔히 "좀 어떠니?"라는 질문을 받을 때 "괜찮아."라고 대답할 것이다. 이것에 대해 단지 '부인'이라고 규정하는 것은 보다 깊은 진실을 놓치는 것이다. 동물이든 사람이든 유기체는 **공격을 피하기 위해** 괜찮아 보이려고 노력할 뿐만 아니라 괜찮은 것은 것으로 노력한다. 이것이 회복 탄력성이 작용되는 것이다.

[해설]

1. 이 글은 "동물이 다쳤을 때 통증을 참고 일어나려는 것은 포식자에게 잡아 먹히지 않기 위해 약한 모습을 보이지 않으려는 것처럼 인간도 비슷하게 힘든 상황에 처할 때 약하게 보이지 않기 위해 괜찮다는 반응을 보인다"는 내용이다. 따라서 빈칸에는 '공격을 피하다'가 가장 적절하다.

2. 주제로는 **a.** "위협에 직면한 동물과 인간의 신체적, 정서적 회복력" 이 적절하다.

[어휘]

instinct 본능 **instinctual** 본능의, 본능적인 **Despite the fact that S+V~** ~라는 사실에도 불구하고 **drive** 몰아붙이다 **alternative** 대안, 다른 방법 **predator** 포식동물, 약탈자 **defenseless** 무방비의, 방어할 수 없는 **devastating** 참담한, 파괴적인 **label** 이름표를 붙이다, ~라고 규정하다 **denial** 부인, 부정; 거부 **organism** 유기체 **resilience** 회복 탄력성 **in action** 작용(작동) 중인 **in the face of ~** 에 직면한, 직면해서 **cope with** ~을 대처하다

4.

Sometimes it is the _____ that gives a business a competitive advantage. Until recently, bicycles had to have many gears, often 15 or 20, for them to be considered high-end. But fixed-gear bikes with minimal features have become more popular, as those who buy them are happy to pay more for much less. The overall profitability of these bikes is much higher than the more complex ones because they do a single thing really well without the cost of added complexity. Companies should be careful of getting into a war over adding more features with their competitors, as this will increase cost and almost certainly reduce profitability because of competitive pressure on price. [고1모의]

— Adapted from Iain Ellwood, *Economist: Marketing for Growth*, 2014

* **high-end** 최고급의

1. 다음 빈칸에 들어갈 말로 가장 적절한 것은?

① simpler product

② affordable price

③ consumer loyalty

④ customized design

2. 이 글의 주제로 가장 적절한 것은?

a. The importance of adding more features for business competitiveness

b. The significance of simplicity in product design for a competitive edge and increased profitability

 Explanations

[해석]

때때로 기업에게 비교우위를 주는 것은 <u>더 단순한 제품</u>이다. 최근까지, 자전거는 최고급이라고 여겨지기 위해서는 보통 15개 혹은 20개의 많은 기어를 가져야 했다. 그러나 최소한의 특징을 가지고 있는, 고정식 기어 자전거들은 그것들을 사는 사람들이 훨씬 적은 것에 대해 기꺼이 더 지불함에 따라 점점 더 인기를 얻게 되었다. 이런 자전거들의 전반적인 수익성은 더 복잡한 것들 보다 훨씬 더 큰데 그것들이 추가되는 복잡성에 대한 비용 없이 한 가지를 정말 잘하기 때문이다. 기업들은 경쟁 업체와 더 많은 특징들을 추가하는 전쟁을 하는 것을 조심해야 하는데, 이것이 가격에 대한 경쟁적인 압박 때문에 비용을 증가시키고 수익성을 거의 확실히 감소시킬 것이기 때문이다.

[해설]

1) 첫 문장이 주제문이 될 수 있다. 이 글의 요지는 "더 단순한 제품이 기업에게 시장에서의 우위와 수익을 가져다 준다" 이다. 그래서 빈칸에는 ① simpler product (더 단순한 제품)이 가장 적절하다.

2) 이글의 주제로는 **b.** "경쟁 우위와 수익성 증대를 위한 제품 설계의 단순성의 중요성"가 적절하다.

[어휘]

competitive advantage = competitive edge 경쟁 우위 **feature** 특징, (제품)편의 장치, 기능 **overall** 전반적인 **profitability** 수익성 **affordable price** 저렴한(구입 가능한) 가격 **consumer loyalty** 소비자 충성도 **customized design** 맞춤형 디자인

5.

As always happens with natural selection, bats and their prey have _____ for millions of years. It's believed that hearing in moths arose specifically in response to the threat of being eaten by bats. (Not all insects can hear.) Over millions of years, moths have evolved the ability to detect sounds at ever higher frequencies, and, as they have, the frequencies of bats' vocalizations have risen, too. Some moth species have also evolved scales on their wings and a fur-like coat on their bodies; both act as "acoustic camouflage," by absorbing sound waves in the frequencies emitted by bats, thereby preventing those sound waves from bouncing back. The B-2 bomber and other "stealth" aircraft have fuselages made of materials that do something similar with radar beams. [고2모의]

— Adapted from David Owen, *Volume Control: Hearing in a Deafening World*, 2020, p. 21

*frequency: 주파수 ****camouflage**: 위장 *****fuselage**: (비행기의) 기체

1. 빈칸에 들어갈 말로 가장 적절한 것은?

① been in a fierce war over scarce food sources

② been engaged in a life-or-death sensory arms race

③ invented weapons that are not part of their bodies

④ evolved to cope with other noise-producing wildlife

⑤ adapted to flying in night skies absent of any lights

2. 이 글의 주제로 가장 적절한 것은?

a. acoustic camouflage in moths: survival strategy

b. adaptive evolution in moths: responses to bat threats

c. stealth techniques in nature and technology: bats, moths, and aircraft

 *Explanations*

[해석]

자연 선택에서 항상 그렇듯이, 박쥐와 그 먹이감은 수백만 년 동안 **생사를 가르는 감각 군비 경쟁에 참여해** 왔다. 나방의 청력은 특히 박쥐에게 잡아 먹히는 위협에 대한 반응으로 생겨난 것으로 여겨진다. (모든 곤충이 들을 수 있는 것은 아니다.) 수백만 년 동안, 나방은 계속 더 높아진 주파수의 소리를 감지하는 능력을 진화시켰고, 나방들이 그렇게 진화함에 따라 박쥐의 발성 주파수도 높아졌다. 일부 나방 종들은 또한 날개에 비늘과 몸에 모피와 같은 코트를 진화시켰다. 둘 다 '음향 위장'의 역할을 하는데, 박쥐에 의해 방출되는 주파수의 음파를 흡수해버린다. 그래서 박쥐가 내는 음파가 반사되어 되돌아가지 못하게 한다. B-2 폭격기와 그 밖의 '스텔스' 항공기도 레이더 빔을 가지고 (나방과 같은) 유사한 역할을 하는 재료로 만들어진 기체를 가지고 있다.

[해설]

1. 빈칸 주론:

빈칸이 있는 첫 번째 문장이 주제문이다. 주제문이 후의 글 내용은 "나방은 박쥐에게 잡아 먹히지 않기 위해 청력이 생겼고 더 높은 주파수 소리를 감지하도록 진화되었다. 그에 따라 박쥐의 발성 주파수도 높아졌다. 일부 나방 종은 날개에 있는 비늘과 신체의 외피를 진화시켜 박쥐 음파를 흡수해서 되돌아 가지 못하게 한다. B-2 폭격기와 '스텔스' 항공기도 나방과 같은 유사한 역할을 하는 동체를 가지고 있다." 이다 그래서 이 글 주제문 내의 빈칸에는 '자연선택설'처럼, 박쥐와 그 먹이감은 수백만 년 동안 **"생사의 감각 군비 경쟁에 참여해왔다"**라는 내용이 가장 적절하다. [정답] ②

2. 이 글의 주제는 **b. adaptive evolution in moths: responses to bat threats** (나방의 적응 진화: 박쥐 위협에 대한 대응)가 적절하다.

[어휘]

natural selection 자연선택, 자연 도태 **be engaged in** ~에 관여(종사, 참여)하다 **sensory** 감각의 **arms race** 군비 경쟁 **hearing** 청력 **arise** 발생하다, 일어나다, 생겨나다 **specifically** 특히, 구체적으로 **in response to** ~에 반응(대응)으로 **frequency** 주파수; 주기, 빈도 **vocalization** 발성 **acoustic** 음향의 **camouflage** 위장 **emit** 발산(방출)하다, 내보내다 **thereby** 그래서, 그로 인해 **adapt to** ~에 적응하다 **adaptive** 적응할 수 있는, 적응하는 **fierce war** 치열한 전쟁 **scarce food sources** 부족한 식량 공급원 **evolve** 진화하다 **evolution** 진화

VOLUME
CONTROL

HEARING IN A
DEAFENING WORLD

DAVID OWEN

6.

Like all animal species (including humans), plants must spread their offspring to areas where they can thrive and pass on their parents' genes. Young animals disperse by walking or flying, but plants don't have that option, so they must somehow hitchhike. While some plant species have seeds adapted for being carried by the wind or for floating on water, many others trick an animal into carrying their seeds, by wrapping the seed in a tasty fruit and advertising the fruit's ripeness by its color or smell. The hungry animal plucks and swallows the fruit, walks or flies off, and then spits out or defecates the seed somewhere far from its parent tree. Seeds can in this manner be carried for thousands of miles.

— Adapted from Jared Diamond, *Guns, Germs, and Steel*, p.110

---

disperse 퍼뜨리다, 전파하다, 뿌리다 pluck [열매 등을] 따다 spit out (침)을 내뱉다 defecate 배변하다

---

1. 위 글의 주제로 가장 알맞은 것은?

a. Animal Behavior and Plant Interaction

b. Seed Dispersal Mechanisms in Plants

c. The Evolutionary Adaptations of Plants

d. The Role of Animals in Plant Reproduction

e. Animals as Seed Dispersal Agents

2. 주어진 단어를 사용하여 요지문을 완성하시오.

Plants employ _____, such as _____

_____, to ensure _____

_____ to favorable locations for _____.

(the spread of their offspring/ optimal germination and growth/ wind dispersal and animal-assisted seed transport/ diverse and ingenious strategies)

요지: 식물은 바람을 통한 분산과 동물의 도움을 통한 씨앗 운송과 같은 다양하고 독창적인 전략을 사용하여 최적의 발아와 성장을 위해 자손이 유리한 위치로 퍼질 수 있도록 한다.

 *Explanations*

[해석]

Plant Reproductive Strategies for Seed Dispersal (종자 분산을 위한 식물 번식 전략)

인간을 포함한 모든 동물 종과 마찬가지로 식물은 번성하고 부모의 유전자를 전달할 수 있는 지역으로 자손을 퍼뜨려야 한다. 어린 동물들은 걷거나 날아서 흩어지지만, 식물은 그런 선택권이 없기 때문에 어떻게든 히치하이킹(hitchhike)을 해야 한다. 일부 식물 종들은 바람에 실려 가거나 물 위에 떠 있는 데 적합한 씨앗을 가지고 있는 반면, 다른 많은 종들은 씨앗을 맛있는 과일로 포장하거나 색깔이나 냄새로 과일이 익었음을 광고함으로써 동물을 속여 씨앗을 옮기게 한다. 굶주린 동물은 열매를 따서 삼키고, 걷거나 날아간 다음, 어미 나무에서 멀리 떨어진 어딘가에서 씨를 뱉아내거나 배설한다. 이런 식으로 씨앗은 수천 마일로 운반될 수 있다.

[해설]

1. 이 글의 주제로 **b. Seed Dispersal Mechanisms in Plants** (식물에서의 씨앗 분산 메커니즘)이 가장 적절하다.

a. Animal Behavior and Plant Interaction (동물 행동과 식물 상호작용)

c. The Evolutionary Adaptations of Plants (식물의 진화적 적응)

d. The Role of Animals in Plant Reproduction (식물 번식에서 동물의 역할)

e. Animals as Seed Dispersal Agents (씨앗 분산제로서의 동물)

2. 이 글의 요지문은 다음과 같다:

Plants employ <u>diverse and ingenious strategies</u>, such as <u>wind dispersal and animal-assisted seed transport</u>, to ensure <u>the spread of their offspring</u> to favorable locations for <u>optimal germination and growth</u>.

요지: 식물은 바람을 통한 분산과 동물의 도움을 통한 씨앗 운송과 같은 다양하고 독창적인 전략을 사용하여 <u>최적의 발아와 성장</u>을 위해 <u>자손이</u> 유리한 위치로 <u>퍼질 수</u> 있도록 한다.

[어휘]

employ ~을 사용하다 **diverse** 다양한(various) **ingenious** 독창적인(creative) **strategy** 전략 **dispersal** 분산, 퍼짐(spread) **offspring** 자손, 후손 **favorable** 우호적인, 유리한 **optimal** 최적의 **germination** (씨앗) 발아 **spread** ~을 확산(분산)시키다, 퍼지게 하다; 확산, 분산, 퍼짐 **offspring** 자손, 후손 **thrive** 번성(번영, 번창)하다 **gene** 유전자 **disperse** 퍼뜨리다, 전파하다, 뿌리다 **adapt** 적응시키다 **trick A into ~ing** A를 속여서 ~하게하다 **ripeness** 성숙 **pluck** [열매 등을] 따다 **spit out** (침)을 내뱉다 **defecate** 배변하다 **evolutionary** 진화의 **adaptation** 적응; 각색 **reproduction** 번식, 생식; 재생산 **agent** 촉매제, 약제; 매개물; 행위자; 요원; 직원

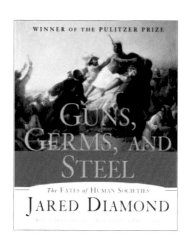

Quote Break

"**M**uch of human history has **consisted of unequal conflicts** between **the haves** and **the have-nots.**"

— Jared Diamond, *Guns, Germs, and Steel: The Fates of Human Societies*, p.89

"인류 역사의 대부분은 가진 자와 가지지 못한 자 사이의 불평등한 갈등으로 이루어져 있다."

[어휘 & 표현]

---

consist of ~로 이루어져 있다 **unequal** 불평등한 **conflict** 갈등, 분쟁 **the haves** 가진 자들, 기득권자들 **the have-nots** 가지지 못한 자들

《**총, 균, 쇠**》(**Guns, Germs & Steel**)로 한국에서도 베스트셀러가 되었고, 1998년 퓰리처상 논픽션 부분을 수상한 21세기의 찰스 다윈(Charles Darwin)이라 불리는 미국의 과학자이자 논픽션작가인 **Jared Diamond**의 명언입니다. 이 글은 5장(History's Haves and Have-nots)의 첫 문장으로 여기서 말하는 불평등한 갈등(unequal conflicts)은 '농업의 힘을 가진 민족들과 그렇지 못한 민족들과의 사이의 갈등 또는 서로 다른 시기에 농업의 힘을 얻은 민족들 사이'의 갈등을 말합니다. Diamond는 농업(식량생산)의 부상이 인류 문화발전에 미치는 영향에 대해 말해주고 있습니다.

Chapter 2

Locations of Main Idea

요지는 어디에 있나요?

What you need to learn:

❝*The only thing that you absolutely have to know*

is the location of the library.❞

– Albert Einstein (1879 – 1955)

2.1. Locations of Main Idea

요지(Main Idea)를 표현하는 주제문(Topic Sentence)은 문단 내 아무 곳에나 나타날 수 있다. 주제문은 문단 내에 있는 모든 또는 대부분의 세부사항들을 아우르는 포괄적 진술(General Statement)이라는 점을 명심하라.

1. Topic Sentence at the Beginning

주제문이 첫 문장인 경우

Topic Sentence

Supporting Detail

Supporting Detail

Supporting Detail

Supporting Detail

필자는 종종 요지를 나타내는 문장을 시작으로 문단을 전개한다. 첫 문장이 주제문으로 문단 전체를 아우르는 포괄적 진술이다. 그리고 문단의 나머지 문장들은 구체적인 이유나 부연설명 또는 사실 등의 세부사항으로 요지를 뒷받침 해준다.

Example: 다음 문단의 주제문을 찾으시오.

[1]Pain can cause aggression. [2]When two rats in the same cage were given foot shocks, they attacked each other immediately. [3]In addtion, stronger shocks resulted in more violent aggression. [4]Pairs of various other animals reacted similarly. [5]A stubbed toe or a headache has been known to cause similar response in humans.

*Topic sentence:*_____

 Explanations

첫 문장이 포괄적인 내용으로 필자의 요지를 제시하는 주제문이다. 나머지 문장들은 구체적인 예를 들어 요지를 뒷받침해 준다.

[어휘] aggression 공격성, 침략 immediately 즉각, 즉시 result in ~을 초래하다(cause) stubbed toe 부딪힌 발가락

2. Topic Sentence Within a Paragraph

주제문이 문단 내에 있는 경우

```
Introductory sentence(s)
Topic Sentence
Supporting Detail
Supporting Detail
Supporting Detail
```

한 문장 이상의 도입부를 가지고 있는 문단으로 도입부 문장은 문단의 Topic 을 소개해주거나 요지에 대한 배경지식을 미리 제공해주는 역할을 한다. 특히 필자는 독자의 관심이나 흥미를 유발하기위해 도입부에 질문이나 명언, 속담, 실험(연구, 조사)결과 또는 통계자료 등을 인용하면서 글을 전개한다. 그런 다음 필자가 Topic 에대해 말하고자 하는 바(요지문 혹은 주제문)를 문단 내에 제시하고 그에 따른 구체적인 이유나 부연설명 또는 사실 등의 세부내용으로 요지를 뒷받침한다.

Example A: 아래 문단의 주제문을 찾아 빈칸에 문장 번호를 쓰시오.

[1]**Why** aren't the letters on a typewriter keyboard in alpahaetical order? [2]The odd letter arrangement on the keyboard was developed over a hundred years ago to solve a problem. [3]The mechanical parts of early typewriters were too slow to keep up with fast typing, which would result in jammed keys. [4]As a result, the designers chose an awkward arrangement of letters for the keyboard. [5]The typist was thus forced to slow down, and the keys didn't jam.

Topic sentence:_____

 Explanations

첫 문장을 질문으로 시작하는 문단이다. 그리고 이 질문에 대한 답이 바로 다음 문장으로 연결되어 있다. 답이 바로 필자의 요지 "The odd letter arrangement was used to solve a problem" 가 될 수 있다. 그리고 나머지 문장들은 그 문제와 해결을 설명하는 세부적 내용들이다.

[어휘] odd letter arrangement 이상한 글자 배열 keep up with ~을 따라가다,~와 (보조)를 맞추다 awkward 어색한

Reversal Transitions 역접 연결어

글의 도입부에 일반적인 다수 견해(Public Opinion)나 잘못된 생각(Common Misconceptions), 주장 또는 사회적 통념(Myth, Conventional Wisdom)이나 논란이 되는 이슈 등을 등을 제시하고 이를 반박하거나 비판하면서 다른 견해나 주장을 전개하는 글을 흔히 볼 수 있다. 이런 구조의 글은 필자의 어조와 논리성이 뚜렷한 글이며 기존 견해나 주장을 반박하는 전환 부분에는 **However, But, Yet** 등과 같은 역접 연결어가 사용된다. 그 전환점을 표시하는 역접 연결어는 문단의 요지(주제문)를 이끄는 역할을 한다.

역접과 대조의 표시어(Signal Words)

아래 표시어의 뜻을 적고 암기하시오.

부사(구)	전치사	접속사
However, Yet, But	despite	**although** S +V ~
conversely, reversibly	**in spite of**	**even though** S+V ~
nevertheless, nonetheless	contrary to	**even if** S+V ~
on the other hand		**while** S+V ~
in contrast, on the contrary		**whereas** S+V ~
Instead, **Rather**, Still		, **but** S+V ~
Unfortunately		
Ironically		
Actually, **In fact**, **In reality**		

Example B: 문단 안에 역접 연결사에 세모를 하고 문단의 주제문을 찾으시오.

[1]Today we take world-wide communications for granted. [2]Through TV, radio, Internet, and celluar phones, we learn almost instantly what happens throughout the world. [3]In Roman times, **however**, military leaders relied on a much slower, less technical method to send important messages back to headquarters – pigeons. [4]Homing pigenons have a strong instinct to return home from just about anywhere. [5]The birds were kept in cages at the military camps. [6]When a message had to be sent, a soldier strapped it to the bird's leg. [7]The birds was then released, and it flew home, delivering the message.

Topic sentence:_____

![Thanks!] **Explanations**

역접 연결사 However 가 있는 3 번째 문장이 주제문이다. 첫 문장과 두번재 문장은 도입 문장으로 오늘닐 우리는 인터넷, TV, 라디오를 통해 세계 도처에 일어나는 일들을 즉각적으로 알게된다는 소개글이다. 그리고 나서 필자는 '로마시대의 지도자들은 메시지 전달 방법으로 귀환 비둘기에 의존했다'는 내용의 글을 전개한다.

[어휘] **take A for granted** A를 당연하게 여기다 **instantly** 즉각적으로 **headquarter** 본부, 본사 **homing pigeon** 귀환 비둘기 **instinct** 본능 **strap** ~을 묶다, 매다

3. Topic Sentence at the End of A paragraph

주제문이 문단 끝에 있는 경우

```
┌─────────────────────────────┐
│      Supporting Detail       │
│                              │
│      Supporting Detail       │
│                              │
│      Supporting Detail       │
│                              │
│      Supporting Detail       │
│                              │
│        Topic Sentence        │
└─────────────────────────────┘
```

이러한 접근 방식의 문단은 세부내용들(Supporting Details)을 통해 필자가 말하고자 하는 바(요지, Main Idea)를 구축할 수 있기 때문에 매우 효과적인 글이다. 이러한 글의 흐름을 귀납적(Inductive)이라고 한다. 글은 세부적인 글에서 포괄적인 글로 이동한다. 문단 끝에 있는 주제문(Topic Sentence)은 문단 내의 모든 세부내용을 요약(Summary)하거나 결론(Conclusion)을 나타내는 문장이다.

귀납적 사고(Inductive Thinking or **Inductive Reasoning** 귀납적 추론)는 특정 세부 사항을 기반으로 일반적인 이해에 도달하는 과정으로, 수학과 과학에서 이론을 도출하거나 세부 사항이 서로 어떻게 연결되는지 탐구하는 데 사용된다. 특히, 귀납적 접근법은 자신의 주장에 동의하도록 설득하려는 정치인이나 또는 제품을 구매하도록 설득하는 상업 광고주들이 이 접근법을 자주 사용한다.

만약 정치인이 "세금을 올려야 한다"는 주장을 연설 시작부터 하면 청중은 강하게 반대할 수도 있고 세금을 올려야 하는 구체적인 이유를 듣지 않을 수도 있다. 그러나 정치인이 세부사항(세금을 올려야만 하는 구체적 이유)에서 시작하여 요지(그래서, 세금을 올려야 한다)로 이어지면 사람들은 더 잘 귀 기울일 것이고 세금 인상에 동의할 수 있을 것이다. 세부적인 것에서 포괄적인 것으로의 이러한 흐름은 창의적인 글쓰기에서도 효과가 있다.

Example A: 주제문을 찾으시오

[1]Albert Einstein was one. [2]So was artist Pablo Picasso. [3]American writer and humorist Mark Twain was one, as well. [4]Others include Babe Ruth, General Norman Schwartzkopf, Johann Sebastian Bach, and Joan of Arc. [5]What do all of these famous people have in common? [6]All of them are left-handed.

Topic sentence: _____

Example B: 주제문을 찾으시오

[1]Studies show that a dog or cat creates a more relaxed home environment, which can help to end family arguments. [2]In addition, pets often serve as an emotional outlet for older men. [3]The men share thoughts and feelings with the pets that they don't share with the rest of the family. [4]Pets also ease life's stressful times, including the death of a loved one. [5]Furthermore, pets have been used with proven success in increasing the will to live among older people. [6]**Clearly**, pets can be good for our mental health.

Topic sentence: _____

Explanations

주제문은 6 번째 문장이다. 구체적인 세부내용들을 들면서 마지막 부분에 포괄적인 문장으로 결론을 도출하는 글이다: 반려동물은 보다 편안한 가정환경에 기여, 노인의 정시적 배출구 역할, 어려운 시기에 스트레스를 완화, 노인의 삶의 의지를 높이는 데 입증되었다. 그래서 반려동물의 존재는 정신 건강에 긍정적인 영향을 미치는 것으로 강조된다.

[어휘] **serve as** ~로 역할을 하다 **outlet** 배출구

결론&결과, 요약, 강조를 나타내는 연결어

아래 연결어들은 일반적으로 문단의 후반부에 위치하며 글 전체 내용을 요약 또는 강조하거나 결론을 이끌어 내는 표시어(Signal Words)들이다. 이러한 표시어가 있는 문장은 종종 필자의 주장이나 글의 요지인 경우가 많으므로 독해 시 '무엇을 요약하는 것인지', 무엇을 강조하는 것인지', '무엇에대한 결론인지'를 파악해야한다.

아래 연결어의 뜻을 적고 암기하시오.

Conclusion & Effect 결론&결과	Summary 요약	Emphasis 강조
In conclusion	In summary	indeed
accordingly	In short	in fact
therefore, hence, thus, so	In brief	actually
consequently	All in all	certainly
as a result	In a word	clearly
For these reasons	In other words	

4. Topic Sentence at the Beginning and the End

주제문이 문단 시작과 끝에 있는 경우

Topic Sentence
Supporting Detail
Supporting Detail
Supporting Detail
Topic Sentence

문단 앞부분에 요지를 말하고나서 필자의 주장을 강조하기위해 문단의 끝부분에 다른 말로 요지를 재언급(restatement)한다.

Example: 아래 문단의 주제문을 찾으시오

[1]New findings from dental research on rats suggest the possibility of creating chocolate that is good for your dental health. [2]In one study, researchers found that rats who ate chocolate candy high in fat and milk protein got 71 percent fewer cavities than those who ate sugar or fudge alone. [3]In a follow-up study, rats were fed cholcolate candy that had an even greater amount of the milk protein. [4]Remarkably, these rats then got almost no cavities at all. [5]Because of this research, a company may develop a chocolate candy that's healthful for your teeth.

Topic sentences: _____

 Explanations

문단의 첫문장에 있는 요지는 마지막 문장에서 다른 말로 재언급(Restatement) 된다.
첫 문장: 쥐를 대상으로 한 치과 연구의 새로운 발견은 치아 건강에 좋은 초콜릿을 만들 수 있는 가능성을 시사한다.
마지막 문장: 이 연구 덕분에, 어떤 회사는 치아에 좋은 초콜릿 캔디를 개발할 수도 있다.

[어휘] cavity 충치 fudge 말랑한 캔디 follow-up study 후속 연구 feed (fed – fed) ~에게 먹이를 주다

5. Topic Sentence Implied

주제문이 없는 경우

```
┌────────────────────────────┐
│      Supporting Detail      │
│      Supporting Detail      │
│      Supporting Detail      │
│      Supporting Detail      │
│      Supporting Detail      │
└────────────────────────────┘
```

가끔 주제문이 없는 문단도 있다. 하지만 주제문이 없다고 해서 이 문단의 요지가 없다는 것은 아니다. 필자가 문단 내에 있는 구체적인 세부내용만으로도 요지를 암시해 주기에 충분하다고 판단했기 때문에 주제문을 제시하지 않았을 뿐이다. 이러한 내포된, 암시된, 혹은 숨은 요지(Implied, suggested, or unstated Main Idea)는 다음 장에서 본격적으로 다룬다.

Guidelines for finding the topic sentence: 주제문을 찾는 3 단계 지침

1st 단계: Identify the topic of the paragraph by asking yourself,

"**What is the paragraph about?**"

2nd 단계: Find the general statement:

"**What is the author's main point about the topic?**"

3rd 단계: Test your answer by asking yourself,

"**Is this general statement supported by all or most of the sentences**

in the paragraph?"

PRACTICE 1

아래 각 문단을 읽고 주제문(Topic Sentence)을 찾고 아래 질문에 답하시오.
반드시 주제문을 찾는 3단계 지침을 따르면서 빨리 독해 할려고 노력하라!

1.

[1]We might like to think of ourselves as so sophisticated that physical attractiveness does not move us. [2]We might like to claim that sensitivity, warmth, and intelligence are more important to us. [3]However, we might never learn about other people's personalities if they do not meet our minimal standards for physical attractiveness.

— Adapted from Spencer A. Rathus, *Psychology and the Challenges of Life*, 2019, p. 301

sophisticated 세련된; 교양있는
claim 주장하다 **sensitivity** 감수성 **intelligence** 지성, 지능; 총명함 **meet** 충족시키다(satisify)

1) 주제문의 위치? _____

2) 글의 주제로 가장 적절한 것을 고르시오.

  a. challenge of learning about other people's personalities

  b. significance of sensitivity, warmth, and intelligence in relationships

  c. influence of physical attractiveness on personal perceptions

2.

[1]A strand of spider's silk is capable of holding five times more weight than a similar strand of steel, making it one of the strongest substances in the world. [2]The silk is also extremely elastic: a strand only four-millionths of an inch in diameter can stretch to twice its original length before breaking. [3]So if it were practical to harvest webs or to milk spiders, the diaphanous material would be ideal for industrial use.

— Adapted from *Discovery*, Vol.10, p.6

---

strand 줄, 실 be capable of ~ing ~을 할 수 있다 elastic 탄력있는, 탄성의 practical 실용적인 harvest 수확하다, 채취하다 milk (젖,체액,독 등을) 짜내다; 이용(착취)하다 diaphanous 매우 얇은 impracticality 비실용성

---

1) 주제문의 위치? _____

2) 글의 주제로 가장 적절한 것을 고르시오.

   a. harvesting spider webs for industrial use

   b. strength of spider silk compared to steel

   c. impracticality of using spider silk

3.

[1]Young women who suffer from *anorexia nervosa*, an eating disorder, severely limit their food intake to the point of significant weight loss and near starvation. [2]Many young women also have *bulimia nervosa*, another serious eating disorder, which involves frequent binges (overeating) followed by purges (self-induced vomiting or the use of laxatives). [3]In the United States approximately 10 million women experience one of these disorders. [4]Both of these life-threatening eating disorders involve an obsessive relationship with food, and women who have these disorders must be treated professionally before they permanently damage their bodies.

---

suffer from (병 등)으로 고생하다, (병)을 겪다 ***anorexia nervosa*** 신경성 식욕부진증(거식증) **disorder** 장애 **intake** 섭취량 **starvation** 굶주림,기아 ***bulimia nervosa*** 신경성 포식증 **self-induced** 자체 유도한 **laxative** 설사약 **obsessive** 강박적인 **premanently** 영구적으로 **prevalence** 만연, 유행; 우세; 유병률

---

1) 주제문의 위치? _____

2) 글의 주제로 가장 적절한 것을 고르시오.

a. relationship between *bulimia* and *anorexia*

b. need for professional treatment for eating disorders

c. prevalence of eating disorders in the United States

4.

¹*Hot* and *cold* are the two main words we use to describe how we perceive temperature. ²They are imprinted on our consciousness at a very early age. ³And for the most part, we have no problem telling the difference between the two. ⁴Yet sometimes the difference isn't altogether clear. ⁵Here's an example: If you were blindfolded and someone touched you first with a hot iron and then with a piece of dry ice, you probably wouldn't be able to tell hot from cold. ⁶This is a simple demonstration of a key fact. ⁷Physiological, or bodily, response isn't a dependable method for measuring temperature. [고 1 모의]

— Adapted from Laraine Femming, *Reading Keys*, p122

perceive 지각하다, 인식하다 be imprinted on ~에 각인되다, 새겨지다 consiousness 의식 blindfold 눈을 가리다
demonstration 증명, 시연, 설명;시위 physiological 생리적인, 생리학상의 dependable 신뢰할 수 있는(reliable)

1) 주제문의 위치? _____

2) 글의 주제로 가장 적절한 것을 고르시오.

a. challenge of differentiating hot and cold through touch

b. reliability of physiological response in measuring temperature

c. blindfolded demonstration of temperature perception

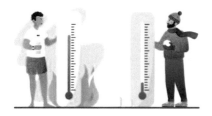

5.

[1]In the United States, Australia, and Western Europe people are encouraged to be independent. [2]Members of these cultures are taught to get ahead, to compete, to win, to achieve their goals, to realize their unique potential, to stand out from the crowd. [3]In many Asian and African countries, people are taught to value an interdependent self. [4]Members of these cultures are taught to get along, to help others, and to not disagree or stand out. [5]Thus, there are significant cultural differences in the way people are taught to view themselves.

— Adapted from Joseph A. DeVito, *Basic Speech*, 1998, p. 81

independent 독립적인, 자립의 **potential** 잠재력 **stand out** 눈에 띠다, 두드러지다
value ~에 가치를 두다, ~을 중시하다 **interdependent** 상호의존적인 **get along** 사이좋게 지내다

1) 주제문의 위치? _____

2) 글의 주제로 가장 적절한 것을 고르시오.

   a. importance of independence in Western cultures

   b. cultural variations in teaching self-perception

   c. achieving personal goals in different cultures

6.

[1]Being a judge may be a lofty job, but judges often face the down-to-earth problem of fighting off sleepiness during a long trial. [2]One reason is that arguments made by attorneys are usually routine. [3]They are also often long and boring. [4]A second reason is that judges are seated all during trials. [5]This can slow the body down, especially after lunch. [6]Also, courtrooms are usually stuffy. [7]Air circulation is poor, and there are no windows. [8]Lighting is dim. [9]These factors all make staying awake during trials a challenging task for judges.

---

lofty 고상한 **down-to-earth** 현실적인, 실제적인 **trial** 재판; 시도 **make arguments** 변론하다 **attorney** 변호사 **routine** 일상, 일과 **be seated** 착석되다 **stuffy** 통풍이 안 되는, 답답한 **air circulation** 공기 순환 **challenging** 힘든, 어려운; 도전적인 **mundane** 평범한, 일상적인; 현세의, 세속의 **alertness** 경계, 주의(환기) **physical strain** 신체적 긴장(부담, 피로) **prolonged** 장시간의, 장기화된

---

1) 주제문 2 개의 위치는? _____

2) 글의 주제로 가장 적절한 것을 고르시오.

　a. challenges faced by judges in staying awake during trials

　b. mundane nature of attorney arguments in court

　c. environmental factors affecting judges' alertness in courtrooms

　d. physical strain of prolonged seating for judges

7.

[1]Our lives have been enriched by inventions we might never have known about without the determination of the products' inventors. [2]In 1939, for example, a professor built the first computer using "base 2", a series that was easy for a machine to identify. [3]He tried to sell his idea to IBM, but was turned down. [4]It took seven years before his idea was accepted and the first general-purpose computer was introduced. [5]Today, all computers use the system he devise. [6]Another example is the copy machine patented in 1939. [7]Its inventor tried to sell his idea to twenty different companies. [8]Because no one was interested then, the first commercial copy machine was not introduced until 1959. [9]Through the persistence of inventors such as these, our lives have been changed.

enrich 풍요롭게하다 determination 결단력 identify ~을 식별하다 trun down 거절하다
devise 고안하다 patented 특허 받은 commercial 상업적인 persistence 끈기, 불굴(의 의지), 고집

1) 주제문 2 개의 위치는? _____

2) 글의 주제로 가장 적절한 것을 고르시오.

   a. impact of inventors on technological advancements

   b. challenges faced by early computer inventors

   c. journey from rejection to acceptance in the world of inventions

   d. persistence and determination in the history of inventors

Training 적용 훈련 문제

다음 글을 일고 아래 물음에 답하시오.

1.

Some drugs have a higher chance of being abused than others. However, it is frequently more useful to classify drug-taking *behavior* than it is to rate the drugs themselves. For example, some people remain social drinkers for life, whereas others become alcoholics within weeks of taking their first drink. In this sense, drug use can be classified as *experimental* short-term use based on curiosity or *compulsive* long-term use based on extreme dependence.

— Adapted from Dennis Coon, *Introduction to Psychology*, 12th ed., 2010, p.158.

1) 역접 연결어에 세모 표시하고 주제문에 밑줄을 치시오.

2) 문단의 요지(Main Idea)로 가장 적절한 것은?

a. It makes more sense to rate drug-taking behavior rather than classifying the actual drugs.

b. There's a big difference between experimental and compulsive drug taking.

 Explanations

[해석]

어떤 약물들은 다른 약물들보다 남용될 가능성이 더 높다. **그러나** 약물 자체를 평가하는 것보다 약물 복용시의 행동을 분류하는 것이 더 유용한 경우가 많다. 예를 들어, 어떤 사람들은 평생 사회적 음주가로 남게 되는 반면, 다른 사람들은 처음 술을 마신 지 몇 주 만에 알코올 중독자가 된다. 이런 의미에서, 약물 복용은 호기심에 근거한 *실험적* 단기 복용 또는 극도의 의존성에 기반한 *강박적* 장기 복용으로 분류될 수 있다.

[해설]

이 글의 요지는 **a.** 가 적절하다:

a. 실제 약물을 분류하는 것보다 약물 복용시의 행동을 평가하는 것이 더 타당하다.

b. 실험적 약물 복용과 강박적 약물 복용에는 큰 차이가 있다.

[어휘]

abuse 남용하다 **classify** ~을 분류하다 **drug-taking behavior** 약물 복용시의 행동 **rate** 평가하다, 등급을 매기다 **social drinker** 사회적 음주가 **alcoholic** 알코올중독자 **experimental** 실험적인 **based on** ~에 근거한, 기반한 **curiosity** 호기심 **compulsive** 강박적인 **extreme** 극도의 **dependence** 의존성 **It makes sense to V ~** ~하는 것이 타당하다, 말이 된다

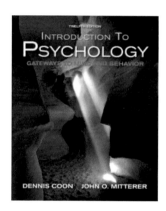

2.

Why do animals hibernate in winter? According to the experts, animals don't hibernate to escape the cold. Rather, hibernating saves energy when food is scarce. For example, during hibernation, a ground squirrel's heart rate falls from a normal 200-400 beats per minute to only 7-10 beats. Because their bodies are so still, the squirrels can simply live off their stored fat. Bears hibernate for the same reason. If they're sleeping, they don't need much energy and don't have to worry about finding food.

1) 역접 연결어에 세모 표시하고 주제문에 밑줄을 치시오.

2) 문단의 요지(Main Idea)로 가장 적절한 것을 고르시오.

a. Animals hibernate in winter in order to lower their heart rate.

b. Animals hibernate in winter to save energy when food is in short supply.

 *Explanations*

|해석|

동물들은 왜 겨울에 겨울잠을 잘까? 전문가들에 따르면, 동물들은 추위를 피하기 위해 겨울잠을 자지 않는다. <u>**오히려**, 겨울잠은 음식이 부족할 때 에너지를 절약한다</u>. 예를 들어, 겨울잠을 자는 동안, 땅다람쥐의 심박수는 분당 정상적인 200-400 회에서 불과 7-10 회로 떨어진다. 다람쥐의 몸은 너무 가만히 있기 때문에 저장된 지방으로 간단히 살 수 있다. 곰들도 같은 이유로 겨울잠을 잔다. 잠을 자고 있으면, 많은 에너지가 필요하지 않으며 음식 찾는 것을 걱정 할 필요가 없다.

|해설|

이 글의 요지는 b.가 적절하다:

a. 동물들은 심박수를 낮추기 위해 겨울에 동면한다.

b. 동물들은 음식이 부족할 때 에너지를 절약하기 위해 겨울에 동면한다.

|어휘|

hibernate 동면하다 **hibernation** 동면, 겨울잠 **scarce** 부족한, 드문 **beat** (심장) 박동 **still** 가만히 있는, 정지한 **stored fat** 저장된 지방 **be in short supply** 부족한 공급 상태에 있다

3.

To some extent, personal identity comes from belonging to social groups. Unfortunately, being part of a larger social group can create problems for minority teenagers. These young people frequently have difficulty defining themselves. Teenagers from African-American, Asian-American, Native-American, and Latino backgrounds often struggle to create a personal identity that combines family values with the values of American society. One tenth-grade Chinese girl who came to America at the age of twelve described her feelings in an essay. Her words perfectly express her struggle for an identity that combines two different worlds: "I don't know who I am. Am I the good Chinese daughter? Or am I an American teenager?"

---

1) 역접 연결어에 세모 표시하고 주제문에 밑줄을 치시오.

2) 이 글의 요지(Main Idea)로 가장 적절한 것은?

 a. For minority teenagers, being part of a larger social group can interfere with identity development.

 b. Asian-American teenagers have a particularly difficult time developing a sense of personal identity.

 *Explanations*

[해석]

어느 정도, 개인적 정체성은 사회적 집단에 속한 것에서 비롯된다. **불행하게도**, 더 큰 사회 집단의 일원이 되는 것은 소수 민족 십대들에게 문제를 일으킬 수 있다. 이 젊은이들은 자주 자신을 정의하는 데 어려움을 겪는다. 아프리카계 미국인, 아시아계 미국인, 원주민 미국인, 그리고 라틴계 미국인 출신의 십대들은 가족의 가치관과 미국 사회의 가치관을 결합하는 개인 정체성을 만들기 위해 힘들게 노력한다. 12 살의 나이에 미국에 온 한 10 학년 중국인 소녀는 글쓰기에서 자신의 감정을 묘사했다. 그녀의 말은 두 개의 다른 세계를 결합하는 하나의 정체성에 대한 그녀의 투쟁(고군분투)을 완벽하게 표현한다: "나는 내가 누군지 모른다. 내가 착한 중국인 딸인가? 아니면 나는 미국인 십대인가?"

[해설]

요지는 **a**. 가 정답:

a. 소수 십대들에게 더 큰 사회적 집단의 일원이 되는 것은 정체성 발달에 방해가 될 수 있다.

b. 아시아계 미국인 십대들은 개인 정체성을 발달시키는데 특히 어려움을 겪는다.

[어휘]

to some extent 어느 정도   **identiy** 정체성   **belong to** ~에 속하다, 소속되다   **monority** 소수(민족, 인종)   **have difficultiy ~ing** ~하는데 어려움을 겪다   **define** 정의(규정)하다   **struggle** 힘들게 노력하다, 고군분투하다; 고군분투, 힘든 노력, 투쟁   **values** 가치관   **interfere with ~** 에 방해가 되다

What is a Social Identity?

Social identity is part of an individual's self-concept that derives from their knowledge of their group memberships.

Social identity theory describes the circumstances under which social identity is more important than personal identity and the ways social identity can influence behavior. The theory was originated by Henri Tajfel and his student, John Turner, in 1979.

4.

For a long time, people have believed that photographs tell us the truth; they show us what really happened. People used to say "Seeing is believing," or "Don't tell me, show me," or even "One picture is worth a thousand words." In courts of law, photographs often had more value than words. These days, however, matters are not so simple. Photographs can be changed by computer; photographs are sometimes false. [수능변형]

1) 역접 연결어에 세모 표시하고 주제문에 밑줄을 치시오.

2) 괄호안에 주어진 단어를 사용하여 요지문을 완성하고 한글로 해석하시오.

Photographs were once believed to _____, but with computer manipulation, they can now _____.

(deceptive/ depict/ be/ truth)

해석: _____

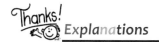

Explanations

[해석]

오랫동안 사람들은 사진이 우리들에게 진실을 말하고 있다고 믿었다. 사진은 우리에게 실제로 일어났던 것을 보여준다. 사람들은 '백문이 불여 일견', 또는 '말로 하지 말고 보여 달라.' 또는 심지어 '사진 한 장이 천 마디 말만큼이나 가치가 있다.'라고 말하곤 했다. 법정에서 사진은 종종 말보다 더 많은 가치를 가지고 있었다. <u>그러나</u> 요즘은 문제가 그렇게 간단하지 않다. <u>사진이 컴퓨터로 변조될 수 있다; 사진은 때때로 가짜이다.</u>

[해설]

이 글은 통념 비판 전개 구조로 다음과 같다:

통념: 사람들은 사진이 진실을 말해 준다고 믿어왔다. **반박**: 사진은 때때로 거짓이다.

글의 요지: 사진은 한때 **진실을 묘사한다**고 믿었지만 컴퓨터 조작으로 이제는 **기만적일 수 있**다.

Photographs were once believed to <u>depict truth</u>, but with computer manipulation, they can now <u>be deceptive</u>.

[어휘]

used to + V ~하곤 했다 **court** 법정, 궁정, 경기장; 구애하다 **value** 가치, 귀중하게 여기다 **matter** 문제, 물질; 중요하다 **valuable** 귀중한 **acceptable** 수용할(받아들일) 수 있는 **false** 거짓인 **deceptive** 거짓의, 허위의; 기만적인 **manipulation** 조작, 조종 **depict** 묘사하다

5.

For centuries there has been a tendency for us to think of health only in terms of physical bodies. The medical community did not look seriously at the possibility that our mind could play an important role in illness and healing. Recently, however, there has been a lot of research that proves our mind affects illness and healing. A medical center reported that a larger portion of their patients were people who did not have an organic disease but were seeking psychological help. [수능변형]

_____

1) 문단에 있는 역접 연결어에 세모 표시하고 주제문에 밑줄을 치시오.

2) 괄호안에 주어진 단어를 사용하여 요지문을 완성하고 한글로 해석하시오.

Recently extensive research has demonstrated that _____

_____.

(both/ our mental state/ illness/ and/ the process of healing/ influences)

해석: _____

 *Explanations*

[해석]

수세기 동안 우리는 신체적인 몸이라는 측면에서만 건강을 생각하는 경향이 있어 왔다. 의학계는 우리의 마음이 병과 치료에 중요한 역할을 할 수 있는 가능성을 진지하게 생각하지 않았다. <u>**그러나**</u> 최근에는 우리 마음이 병과 치료에 영향을 미친다는 것을 증명하는 많은 연구가 있다. 어떤 의료 기관에서는 환자의 반 이상이 어떤 신체 기관의 병을 가지고 있는 것이 아니라 심리적인 도움을 찾으려는 사람들이라고 보고했다.

[해설]

이 글은 통념 반박 전개 구조로 다음과 같다:

통념: 과거에는 신체적인 몸이라는 측면에서만 건강을 생각하는 경향이 있어 왔다. **반박**: 그러나 최근에는 마음이 병과 치료에 영향을 미친다.

글의 요지: 최근 광범위한 연구는 <u>**우리의 정신 상태가 질병과 치유 과정 모두에 영향을 미친다**</u>는 것을 보여주었다.

[정답] <u>our mental state influences both illness and the process of healing</u>

[어휘]

tendency 경향, 추세 **in terms of** ~의 관점에서 **play an important role in** ~에 중요한 역할을 하다 **heal** 치료하다 **a larger portion of** ~ (아주) 많은 **organic** (신체) 기관의, 장기의 **psychological** 심리적인

6.

Most of us believe that we can trust in technology to solve our problems. Whatever problem you name, you can also name some hoped-for technological solution. Some of us have faith that we shall solve our dependence on fossil fuels by developing new technologies for hydrogen engines, wind energy, or solar energy. Some of us have faith that we shall solve our food problems with genetically modified crops newly or soon to be developed. Those with such faith assume that the new technologies will ultimately succeed, without harmful side effects. However, there is no basis for believing that technology will not cause new and unanticipated problems while solving the problems that it previously produced. [수능변형]

---

1) 문단에 있는 역접 연결어에 세모 표시하고 주제문에 밑줄을 치시오.

2) 괄호안에 주어진 단어를 사용하여 요지문을 완성하고 한글로 해석하시오.

While many believe in technology as a solution to various problems, there is no guarantee that _____.

(addressing/ new technologies/ won't cause/ while/ unforeseen issues/ existing problems)

해석: _____

 *Explanations*

[해석]

우리들 대부분은 우리들의 문제를 해결함에 있어서 과학기술을 신뢰할 수 있다고 생각한다. 당신이 어떤 문제를 제기하든 간에 당신은 또한 그에 대한 과학기술적으로 기대할 만한 해결책을 제기할 수 있다. 우리들 중 일부는 수소엔진, 풍력에너지, 또는 태양에너지를 얻기 위한 새로운 기술을 개발함으로써 화석연료에 대한 의존을 해결할 거라는 믿음을 가지고 있다. 우리들 중 일부는 새로이 또는 머지않아 개발될 유전자 변형 곡물로 식량문제를 해결할 거라는 믿음을 가지고 있다. 그러한 믿음을 가진 사람들은 새로운 과학기술이 해로운 부작용 없이 결국 성공을 거두리라고 추측한다. <u>그러나</u> 과학기술이 이전에 발생한 문제를 해결하는 과정에서 새로운 예기치 못한 문제를 야기하지 않을 거라고 믿을 만한 근거는 전혀 없다.

[해설]

이 글은 통념 비판 전개 구조로 다음과 같다:

통념: 과학기술이 인간의 모든 문제를 해결해 주리라는 일부 사람들의 낙관적인 생각

반박: 과학기술이 이전에 발생한 문제를 해결하는 과정에서 새로운 예기치 못한 문제를 야기시킬 수 있다.

글의 요지: 많은 사람들이 기술을 다양한 문제에 대한 해결책이라고 믿지만, <u>새로운 기술이 기존 문제를 해결하면서 예상치 못한 문제를 일으키지 않을 것</u>이라는 보장은 없다

[정답] <u>new technologies won't cause unforeseen issues while addressing existing problem</u>

[어휘]

hoped-for 기대되는 **genetically modified** 유전자 변형의 **assume** 추측하다, 가정하다 **ultimately** 결국, 궁극적으로 **side effect** 부작용 **There is no basis for** ~ 에 대한 근거는 전혀 없다 **unanticipated** 예기치 못한 **misconception** 잘못된 생각, 오해 **address** 다루다, 해결하다(solve) **unforeseen** 예기치 않은(unexpected) **existing** 현존하는, 기존의

Challenge 1등급 도전

문단의 주제문에 밑줄을 치고 아래 물음에 답하시오.

1.

The last two decades of research on the science of learning have shown conclusively that we remember things better, and longer, if _____ _____. This is the teaching method practiced by physics professor Eric Mazur. He doesn't lecture in his classes at Harvard. Instead, he asks students difficult questions, based on their homework reading, that require them to pull together sources of information to solve a problem. Mazur doesn't give them the answer; instead, he asks the students to break off into small groups and discuss the problem among themselves. Eventually, nearly everyone in the class gets the answer right, and the concepts stick with them because they had to find their own way to the answer. [고1모의]

— Adapted from Daniel J. Levitin, *The Organized Mind*, 2nd ed., 2014, p. 367

---

1. 다음 빈칸에 들어갈 말로 가장 적절한 것은?

① they are taught repeatedly in class

② we fully focus on them without any distractions

③ equal opportunities are given to complete tasks

④ there's no right or wrong way to learn about a topic

⑤ we discover them ourselves rather than being told them

2. 이 글의 주제로 가장 적절한 것은?

a. effectiveness of collaborative problem-solving for memory retention

b. benefits of self-discovery in learning and memory retention

Explanations

[해석]

학습과학에 관한 지난 20년간의 연구는 만약 <u>우리가 무언가에 관해서 듣는 것보다 스스로 그것들을 발견한다</u>면 우리는 더 잘 기억하고, 더 오래 기억한다는 것을 결론적으로 보여주었다. 이것은 물리학 교수 Eric Mazur에 의해 실천되는 교수법이다. 그는 하버드 수업에서 (설명식) 강의를 하지 않는다. 대신에, 그는 독서 활동 과제에 기반하여 학생들에게 문제를 해결하기 위해 정보 자료를 모을 수 있게 만드는 어려운 질문을 던진다. Mazur는 그들에게 답을 주지 않는다. 대신에, 그는 학생들을 소그룹으로 나누어 그들 스스로 문제를 토론하도록 요구한다. 결국, 학급의 거의 모든 사람들이 정답을 맞히고, 그들이 정답으로 가는 길을 스스로 찾았기 때문에 이러한 개념들은 그들에게 오래 남는다.

[해설]

1) 첫 문장이 주제문이다. 이 글의 요지를 "<u>Individuals remember information better and longer when they discover it themselves rather than being explicitly told.</u>" (개인은 명시적으로 듣는 것보다 스스로 발견했을 때 정보를 더 잘 기억하고 더 오래 기억한다.)로 표현할 수 있다. 그러므로 빈칸은 ⑤번이 정답이다.

2) 이 글의 주제는 b. "학습과 기억 유지에서 자기 발견의 이점"이며 a. "기억 유지를 위한 협력적 문제 해결의 효과"는 주제가 될 수 없다.

[어휘]

conclusively 결론적으로 **based on** ~에 근거로, ~에 기반하여 **pull together** 모으다 **break off into** ~로 쪼개다, 나누다 **eventually** 결국, 궁극적으로 **implicitly** 암시적으로, 암묵적으로 **explicitly** 명시적으로 **immersion** 몰입 **stick with** ~에 달라붙다, 오래 남다 **distraction** (주의) 산만 **effectiveness** 효과 **collaborative** 협업의, 합작의 **memory retention** 기억 보유(유지); 기억력

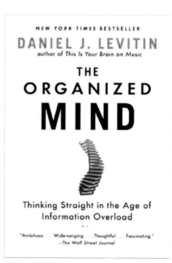

3 Ways to Learn Informaton

There are three ways we can learn information—we can absorb it **implicitly**, we can be told it **explicitly**, or we can discover it ourselves. Implicit learning, such as when we learn a new language through **immersion**, is usually the most efficient. In classroom settings and at work, most information is conveyed in one of the two latter ways—being told explicitly or discovering ourselves. — P. 367

정보를 배울 수 있는 세 가지 방법이 있다. 정보를 <u>**암묵적으로 흡수**</u>하거나, <u>**명시적으로 듣거나**</u>, 또는 <u>**우리 스스로 발견하는 것**</u>이다. 몰입을 통해 새로운 언어를 배우는 것과 같은 암묵적 학습은 일반적으로 가장 효율적이다. 교실 환경과 직장에서 대부분의 정보는 후자의 두 가지 방법 중 하나로 전달된다. 즉, 명시적으로 듣거나 스스로 발견하는 것이다.

2.

There is a famous Spanish proverb that says, "The belly rules the mind." This is a clinically proven fact. Food is the original mind-controlling drug. Every time we eat, we bombard our brains with a feast of chemicals, triggering an explosive hormonal chain reaction that directly influences the way we think. Countless studies have shown that the positive emotional state induced by a good meal _____. It triggers an instinctive desire to repay the provider. This is why executives regularly combine business meetings with meals, why lobbyists invite politicians to attend receptions, lunches, and dinners, and why major state occasions almost always involve an impressive banquet. Churchill called this "dining diplomacy," and sociologists have confirmed that this principle is a strong motivator across all human cultures. [고1모의]

— Adapted from Struan Stevenson, *Course of History: Ten Meals That Changed the World*, 2017, Introduction

* **banquet**: 연회

1. 다음 빈칸에 들어갈 말로 가장 적절한 것은?

① leads us to make a fair judgement

② interferes with cooperation with others

③ does harm to serious diplomatic occasions

④ plays a critical role in improving our health

⑤ enhances our receptiveness to be persuaded

2. 이 글의 주제로 가장 적절한 것은? (2개를 선택하시오)

a. Spanish proverb about the influence of the belly on the mind

b. key to enhancing people's receptiveness: providing a good meal

c. benefits of combining business meetings with meals for executives

d. impact of food on the human mind and its role in social and diplomatic contexts

 Explanations

[해석]

'배가 마음을 다스린다.'라고 하는 유명한 스페인 속담이 있다. 이것은 임상적으로 증명된 사실이다. 음식은 원래 마음을 지배하는 약이다. 우리가 먹을 때마다 우리는 자신의 두뇌에 화학 물질의 향연을 퍼부어 우리가 생각하는 방식에 직접적으로 영향을 미치는 폭발적인 호르몬의 연쇄 반응을 유발한다. 수많은 연구는 좋은 식사로 유발된 긍정적인 감정 상태가 <u>우리의 설득되는 수용성을 높인다</u>는 것을 보여줘 왔다. 그것은 그 제공자에게 보답하려는 본능적인 욕구를 유발한다. 이것이 경영진이 정기적으로 업무 회의와 식사를 결합하는 이유이고, 로비스트들이 정치인들을 리셉션, 점심 식사, 저녁 식사에 참석하도록 초대하는 이유이고, 주요 국가 행사가 거의 항상 인상적인 연회를 포함하는 이유이다. Churchill은 이것을 '식사 외교'라고 불렀고, 사회학자들은 이 원리가 모든 인류 문화에 걸쳐 강력한 동기 부여물이라는 것을 확인해 주어 왔다.

[해설]

1) 빈칸 문장이 문단의 주제문이다. 이 글의 요지는 "<u>좋은 식사로 인한 긍정적인 감정 상태는 그 제공자에게 보답하려는 본능적 욕구를 유발시켜 수용성을 높이기 때문에 정치, 경영, 외교 등에 널리 사용된다.</u>" 이다. 그러므로 빈칸은 ⑤가 가장 적절하다.

2) 이 글의 주제로는 **b. "사람들의 수용성을 높이는 비결: 좋은 식사 제공하기"** 와 **d. "음식이 인간의 마음에 미치는 영향과 사회적, 외교적 맥락에서 음식의 역할"**이다.

[어휘]

clinically 임상적으로 **bombard A with ~** A를 ~ 로 폭격하다, 퍼 붓다 **feast** 향연, 연회 **chemicals** 화학 물질 **trigger** 촉발시키다 **explosive** 폭발적인; 폭발물 **chain reaction** 연쇄 반응 **induce** 유도하다 **instinctive** 본능적인 **instinct** 본능 **repay** 갚다, 보답하다 **executive** 경영자, 책임자; 대표 **state occasions** 국가 행사 **diplomacy** 외교 **diplomatic occasions** 외교 행사 **enhance** 강화하다, 향상시키다 **sociologist** 사회학자 **receptiveness** 수용성 **confirm** 확인하다 **principle** 원리, 원칙 **motivator** 동기유발물 **interfere with** 간섭하다, 방해하다 **context** 상황, 맥락

3.

Here's the unpleasant truth: we are all biased. Every human being is affected by unconscious biases that lead us to make incorrect assumptions about other people. Everyone. To a certain extent, bias is a(n) _____. If you're an early human, perhaps *Homo Erectus*, walking around the jungles, you may see an animal approaching. You have to make very fast assumptions about whether that animal is safe or not, based solely on its appearance. The same is true of other humans. You make split-second decisions about threats in order to have plenty of time to escape, if necessary. This could be one root of our tendency to categorize and label others based on their looks and their clothes. [고1모의]

---

1. 다음 빈칸에 들어갈 말로 가장 적절한 것은?

① necessary survival skill

② origin of imagination

③ undesirable mental capacity

④ barrier to relationships

⑤ challenge to moral judgment

2. 이 글의 제목으로 가장 적절한 것은?

a. Unconscious Biases: A Necessary Survival Skill in Human Evolution Based on External Clues

b. Unconscious Biases: Evolutionary Survival Instincts Based on Inherent Objectivity

 *Explanations*

[해석]

여기 불편한 진실이 있다. 즉, 우리는 모두 편향되어 있다. 모든 인간은 다른 사람들에 대한 부정확한 추측을 하도록 이끄는 무의식적인 편견에 의해 영향을 받는다. 모두가 그렇다. 어느 정도, 편견은 **필수적인 생존 기술이다**. 만약에 당신이, 가령 Homo Erectus처럼, 정글을 돌아다니는 초기 인류라면, 당신은 동물이 다가오는 것을 볼지 모른다. 당신은 그 동물의 외양에만 기초하여 그 동물이 안전한지 아닌지에 대해서 매우 빨리 추측해야 한다. 이것은 다른 인류에게도 똑같이 적용된다. 당신은 만약 필요하다면, 도망갈 많은 시간을 갖기 위하여 위협에 대해서 순간적인 결정을 내려야 한다. 이것은 타인의 외모와 옷으로 그들을 범주화하고 분류하는 성향의 한 근간일지 모른다.

[해설]

1) 빈칸 문장이 이 글의 주제문이다. 이 글의 요지는 '**편견은 생존을 위해 그리고 다른 사람을 판단하는 데 있어서 어느 정도 필수적이다.**'이다. 그러므로 빈칸은 ①이 가장 적절하다.

2) 이 글의 제목은 a. "**무의식적 편견: 외부 단서를 기반으로 한 인간 진화에 필요한 생존 기술**"이다. b. "무의식적 편견: 내재적 객관성에 기초한 진화적 생존 본능" 은 제목이 될 수 없다.

[어휘]

biased 편향된 **bias** 편견 **unconscious** 무의식적인 **assumption** 추측 **To a certain extent** 어느 정도로 **solely** 오로지, 다만 **be true of** ~ 에게 해당되다 **split-second** 순간적인 **tendency** 경향, 성향, 추세 **categorize** 범주화 하다 **label** 분류하다 **undesirable** 바람직하지 않은 **capacity** 능력 **barrier** 장벽 **moral** 도덕적인 **evolution** 진화 **evolutionary** 진화의 **external clues** 외부적 단서들 **survival instinct** 생존 본능 **inherent** 내재된, 타고난 **objectivity** 객관성

4.

Everything in the world around us was finished in the mind of its creator before it was started. The houses we live in, the cars we drive, and our clothing—all of these began with an idea. Each idea was then studied, refined and perfected before the first nail was driven or the first piece of cloth was cut. Long before the idea was turned into a physical reality, the mind had clearly pictured the finished product. The human being designs his or her own future through much the same process. We begin with an idea about how the future will be. Over a period of time, we refine and perfect the vision. Before long, our every thought, decision and activity are all working in harmony to bring into existence what we _____.

[고1모의]

— Adapted from Jim Rohn, *The Five Major Pieces to the Life Puzzle*, p. 27-8

*refine: 다듬다

1. 다음 빈칸에 들어갈 말로 가장 적절한 것은?

① didn't even have the potential to accomplish

② have mentally concluded about the future

③ haven't been able to picture in our mind

④ considered careless and irresponsible

⑤ have observed in some professionals

2. 이 글의 제목으로 가장 적절한 것은?

a. Creative Thinking and Future Design

b. From Idea to Reality: The Process of Human Future Design

c. Bringing Reality to Life Through Creative Reasoning

d. Thoughts Shape Reality: Creativity and Future Planning

 *Explanations*

[해석]

우리 주변 세상의 모든 것은 시작되기 전에 그것을 만들어 낸 사람의 마음속에서 완성되었다. 우리가 사는 집, 우리가 운전하는 자동차, 우리의 옷, 이 모든 것이 아이디어에서 시작했다. 각각의 아이디어는 그런 다음, 첫 번째 못이 박히거나 첫 번째 천 조각이 재단되기 전에, 연구되고, 다듬어지고, 완성되었다. 그 아이디어가 물리적 실체로 바뀌기 훨씬 전에 마음은 완제품을 분명하게 그렸다. 인간은 거의 같은 과정을 통해 자신의 미래를 설계한다. 우리는 미래가 어떨지에 대한 아이디어로 시작한다. 일정 기간에 걸쳐서 우리는 그 비전을 다듬어 완성한다. 머지않아, 우리의 모든 생각과 결정 그리고 활동들이 조화를 이루어 **미래에 대해 우리가 마음속으로 결론을 내린** 것을 생겨나게(실현되게) 한다.

[해설]

1) 빈칸이 있는 마지막 문장이 이 글의 주제문에 가깝다. 이 글의 요지는 세상의 모든 사물이 제작되기 전에 이미 마음속에서 아이디어로 시작해 완성되는 과정처럼 "인간도 창의적인 아이디어를 다듬고 생각, 결정, 행동을 조율하여 자신이 마음속으로 상상한 것을 실현함으로써 자신의 미래를 만들어 나간다."이다. 그러므로 빈칸에 들어갈 말로 ② 가 가장 적절하다.

2) 이 글의 제목으로 b. "아이디어에서 현실로: 인류 미래 설계 과정"가 가장 적절하다.

[어휘]

refine 다듬다, 정제하다 **perfect** ~을 완성시키다 **drive** (못·말뚝 등을) 박다 **physical reality** 물리적 실체(현실) **picture** 그리다, 상상하다 **finished product** 완제품 **bring A into existence** A를 생겨나게 하다, A를 실현하다

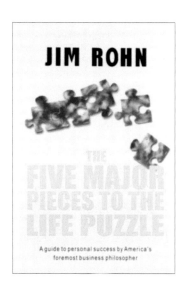

5.

Not only individual organisms are seen today as data-processing systems, but also entire societies such as beehives, bacteria colonies, forests and human cities. Economists increasingly interpret the economy too as a data-processing system. Laypeople believe that the economy consists of peasants growing wheat, workers manufacturing clothes, and customers buying bread and underpants. Yet experts see the economy as a mechanism for gathering data about desires and abilities, and turning this data into decisions.

— Adapted from Yuval Noah Harari, *Homo Deus*, p.430

organism 유기체 **interpret** 해석하다 **laypeople** 일반 사람들 **consist of** ~로 구성되다 **peasant** 농부

1. 위 글의 주제로 가장 알맞은 것은?

a. evolution of organisms and societies

b. data-processing systems in societies

c. interpretation of the economy by economists

d. paradigm shift in perceptions of organisms and societies

2. 주어진 단어를 사용하여 요지문을 완성하시오.

There is a paradigm shift in how organisms, societies, and economies _____

_____, which emphasizes

_____.

(the gathering and utilizing the data/ are perceived/ for decision-making/ as data-processing systems)

요지: 유기체, 사회, 경제를 데이터 처리 시스템으로 인식하는 방식에 패러다임의 전환이 있으며, 이는 의사 결정을 위한 데이터 수집 및 활용을 강조한다.

 *Explanations*

[해석]

오늘날 개별 유기체들 뿐만 아니라 벌집, 박테리아 군집, 숲, 그리고 인간 도시와 같은 사회 전체를 데이터 처리 시스템으로 본다. 경제학자들은 점점 경제도 또한 데이터 처리 시스템으로 해석한다. 일반인들은 경제는 밀을 재배하는 농부들, 옷을 생산하는 노동자들, 그리고 빵과 속옷을 사는 고객들로 구성된다고 믿는다. 그러나 전문가들은 경제를 욕망과 능력에 대한 데이터를 수집해서 이러한 데이터를 의사 결정으로 전환하는 메커니즘으로 본다.

[해설]

1. 이 글의 주제로 **d. Paradigm shift in perceptions of organisms and societies** (유기체와 사회의 인식에 대한 패러다임 전환) 이 가장 적합하다.

a. Evolution of organisms and societies (유기체와 사회의 진화)

b. Data-processing systems in societies (사회에서의 데이터 처리 시스템)

c. Interpretation of the economy by economists (경제학자들의 경제 해석)

2. 이 글의 요지문은 아래와 같다:

There is a paradigm shift in how organisms, societies, and economies <u>are perceived as data-processing systems</u>, which emphasizes <u>the gathering and utilizing the data for decision-making</u>.

요지: 유기체, 사회, 경제를 <u>데이터 처리 시스템으로 인식하는</u> 방식에 패러다임의 전환이 있으며, 이는 <u>의사 결정을 위한 데이터 수집 및 활용</u>을 강조한다.

[어휘]

not only A but (also) B A뿐만 아니라 B도 **individual** 개별의, 개인의; 개인 **beehive** 벌집 **colony** (생물) 군집, 집단; 식민지 **organism** 유기체, 생물; 인간 **interpret** 해석하다 **laypeople** 일반 사람들 **consist of** ~로 구성되다 **peasant** 농부 **evolution** 진화 **interpretation** 해석; 통역 **paradigm shift** 패러다임 전환 **perception** 인식, 인지, 지각 **utilize** 활용하다

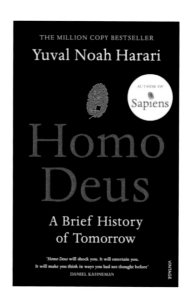

Quote Break

J.K. Rowling은 2008년 하버드 대학교 졸업식 연설에서 실패의 변형적인 힘(transformative power of failure)에 대해 말합니다. 성공적인 작가가 되기 전에 첫 번째 결혼의 실패, 편부모가 되는 것, 가난하게 사는 것을 포함하여 그녀가 직면한 개인적인 역경과 실패 그리고 도전에 대해 이야기합니다. 롤링은 이러한 어려움과 도전이 내면의 힘과 회복력을 개발하는 데 어떻게 도움이 되었으며 궁극적으로 작가로서의 성공으로 이어졌는지를 말해줍니다. 그녀는 실패가 강력한 교사가 될 수 있으며 우리 자신과 주변 세계를 더 깊이 이해하는 데 도움이 된다고 강조합니다.

"It is impossible to live without failing at something, **unless** you live so **cautiously** that you **might as well** not have lived at all – in which case, you fail **by default**."

"무언 가에 실패하지 않고 사는 것은 불가능합니다 — 차라리 아예 살지 않는 편이 더 나을 정도로 그렇게 조심스럽게 살지 않는 한 말입니다. 하지만 이런 경우에도 당신은 기본적으로 실패하기 마련입니다." (도전하지 않고 매우 안정적으로만 사는 삶은 실패한 인생이다)

"Failure gave me an **inner security** that I had never **attained** by passing examinations. Failure taught me things about myself that I could have learned **no other way**. I discovered that I had **a strong will**, and more **discipline** than I had **suspected**; I also found out that I had friends whose value was truly above the price of rubies."

"실패는 나에게 시험을 통과해서는 결코 얻을 수 없는 내면의 안정을 주었습니다. 실패는 나 자신에 대해 어떤 다른 방법으로는 배울 수 없었던 것들을 가르쳐 주었습니다. 나는 내가 생각했던 것보다 강한 의지와 더 많은 규율을 가지고 있다는 것을 발견했습니다. 나는 또한 진정으로 루비보다 가치가 높은 친구들이 있다는 것도 알게 되었습니다."

[어휘 & 표현]

unless S+V ~ 하지 않으면 **cautiously** 조심스럽게 **might as well** + V ~ (차라리)~하는 게 좋겠다, ~하는 편이 낫다 **by default** 기본 설정으로, 기본적으로 **inner security** 내면의 안정(안전) **attain** ~을 달성하다, 얻다 **by passing examination** 시험을 통과함으로써 **no other way** 어떤 다른 방법으로는 ~ 않다 **a strong will** 강한 의지 **discipline** 규율, 훈육; 훈련; 학문(분야) **suspect** 생각하다, 의심하다

Chapter 3

Implied Main Idea

암시된 요지를 찾아라!

What you need to learn:

"An inference is a statement about the unknown

made on the basis of the known."

"추론은 알려진 것을 근거로 미지의 것에 대한 진술이다."

— S. I. Hayakawa, *Language in Thought and Action*

" *The greatest progress* *that the human race has made* *lies in learning how to make correct* <u>*inferences*</u>. "

"인류가 이룩한 가장 위대한 진보는 올바른 추론을 하는 방법을 배우는 데 있다."

─ Friedrich Nietzsche (1844–1900)

3.1. What is an "Implied Main Idea?"

암시된 요지란?

Supporting Detail
Supporting Detail
Supporting Detail
Supporting Detail
Supporting Detail

가끔 주제문이 없는 문단도 있다. 하지만 주제문이 없다고 해서 이 문단의 요지가 없다는 것은 아니다. 필자가 문단내에 있는 구체적인 세부내용만으로도 요지를 암시해 주기에 충분하다고 판단했기 때문에 주제문을 제시하지 않았을 뿐이다. 이 장에서는 이러한 내포된, 암시된, 숨은 요지(Implied, suggested, or unstated Main Idea)를 찾아 내는 독해 기술을 배우고 훈련한다.

A Method for Figuring Out Implied Idea 암시된 요지 찾는 방법

세부 사항(Supporting details)을 살펴보면 암시된 요지를 파악할 수 있다. 이 암시된 요지를 찾아내고자 할 때는 다음과 같은 3 가지의 질문을 자신에게 해야 한다.

1st Q: What is the paragraph about? → *Topic*

2nd Q: What is the main point the author trying to make about the topic?
　　　　→ *Main Idea*

3rd Q: Does all or most material in the paragraph support this Main Idea?

Example A: 다음 글의 암시된 요지는 무엇인지 추론해보라?

You have just adopted a shepherd puppy from an animal shelter. He's lovable but nervous. Whenever you raise your voice for any reason, he immediately becomes fearful and trembles. Even when you scold him, he instinctively hides. When you first brought him from the shelter, he had a slight limp and a noticeable scratch across his nose.

Main Idea: The adopted dog may have been _____ by a previous owner.

 Explanations

3 Questions!

1st Q: **What** is this paragraph **about?** → *Topic*

문단의 모든 문장들은 입양된 강아지에 관한 내용이다. 따라서 문단의 Topic은 Adopted puppy이다.

2nd Q: **What** is the **main point** the author trying to make about the topic?

입양된 강아지의 행동과 외모에 대한 설명들은 입양되기 전에 나쁜 경험을 겪었던 것으로 암시된다: nervous, becomes fearful and trembles, hides, had a slight limp and a scratch across his nose. 등의 근거로 <u>이전 주인으로부터 학대를 당했던 것으로</u> 추론할 수 있다.

3rd Q: **Does** all or most material in the paragraph **support** this Main Idea?

Yes, 입양된 강아지에 대한 모든 세부내용들은 요지를 뒷받침한다.

105

Example B: 다음 문단은 문단 전체의 내용을 포함하는 "우산 개념"의 주제문 (Topic Sentence)이 제시 되어있지 않다. 문단을 읽고 주어진 질문에 답하시오.

On a recent hike in the woods, I was stung by a hornet. As I tried to get away from the hornet, I fell into a thorn bush and scratched my arms. Then I got lost and had to walk an extra four miles before I found the trail. At one point I walked into a patch of shrubs which turned out to be poison ivy. Finally, I was drenched by a sudden rain shower as I was walking back to my car.

1. *The topic of this paragraph is:*

    a. hiking.

    b. getting hurt while on a hike.

    c. a hike in the woods.

2. *The implied main idea of this paragraph is:*

    a. It's easy to get lost while hiking in the woods.

    b. Never go hiking into the woods alone.

    c. The author's hike in the woods was unpleasant.

 Explanations

3 Questions!

1st Q: **What is this paragraph about? → *Topic***

    c. *a hike in the woods*: 문단의 모든 문장들은 숲속에서의 하이킹에 관한 내용들이다. 따라서 문단의 Topic 은 '숲속에서의 하이킹'이다.

2nd Q: **What is the main point the author trying to make about the topic?**

    "Topic 에 대한 필자가 말하고자 하는 바는 무엇인가?" 즉, '숲속에서의 하이킹'(hike in the woods)에 대해서 필자가 말하고자 하는 바는 무엇인가? 해답은 반드시 문단의 모든 세부내용들을 포함하는 포괄적 내용이여야 한다. 그래서 정답은 C 이다. The author's hike in the woods was unpleasant: 문단의 모든 세부내용들은 <u>필자가 하이킹하는 동안에 발생한 불쾌한 문제점들에 관해서 말하고 있다</u>. 이것이 문단의 암시된 요지이다.

3rd Q: **Does all or most material in the paragraph support this Main Idea?**

    Yes, 모든 세부내용들은 요지를 뒷받침해준다.

3.2. Step-by-Step Guide

문단의 암시된 요지를 찾기 위해서 여러분은 형사(detective)가 되어야 한다. 문단의 모든 세부 내용들(Supporting details)을 면밀히 조사한 다음 이러한 세부적인 "증거"들을 이용해서 Topic을 찾고 그 다음 필자가 이 Topic에 대해 말하고자 하는 바가 무엇인지 추론해야 한다. 암시된 요지를 찾기 위해서는 체계적인 독해 훈련이 필요하다. 다음의 5 단계 독해 연습은 암시된 요지를 파악하는데 많은 도움이 될 것이다. 단계별로 하나씩 연습해 보자.

STEP 1. 암시된 포괄적 내용(Implied General Idea) 찾기

아래의 Specific idea 를 가장 잘 포함하는 General idea 에 동그라미 표시를 하시오.

1. *Specific ideas*: retirement, marriage, graduation, funeral
   General idea is:

   a. parties.   b. popular events.   c. *major life events.*

2. *Specific ideas*: eyeglasses, telescope, microscope, magnifying glass
   General idea is:

   a. inventions.   b. very recent inventions.   c. inventions for seeing.

3. *Specific ideas*: "It doesn't fit"   "I don't like the color"   "This tastes like paste"   "Can't you get it right just once?"
   General idea is:

   a. comments.   b. guesses.   c. complaints.

4. *Specific ideas*: "I overslept."   "I missed my bus."   "My watch stopped." "I got caught in a traffic jam."
   General idea is:

   a. comments.   b. explanations.   c. explanations for being late.

STEP 2. 암시된 포괄적 내용(Implied General Idea) 직접 쓰기

세부적인 항목을 포함하는 암시된 포괄적 내용을 빈칸에 직접 적어라.

1. General idea: Parts of a _____
   Specific idea: cover

          table of contents

          chapters

          index

2. General idea: ways of _____
   Specific idea: fried

          hard-boiled

          scrambled

          poached

3. General idea: Jobs in a _____
   Specific idea: chef

          waitress

          cashier

          bus boy

4. General idea: things that are _____
   Specific idea: snow

          wedding dress

          milk

          the President's house in U.S.

5. General idea: ways to _____
   Specific idea: pay attention in class

          take good notes

          keep up with your homework

          hand in papers on time

STEP 3. 암시된 요지(Implied Main Idea) 찾기

암시된 요지는 "너무 광범위한"(too broad) 내용이 되어서도 안 되고 "너무 좁은"(too narrow) 내용이 되어서도 안 된다. 요지는 문단속에 있는 모든 세부 내용을 다 포함하는 "포괄적 진술(General Statement)"이다.

Example: 아래 세부적 진술들을 모두 포괄하는 요지를 고르시오.

1. Men accuse women of not trusting them.

2. Men complain that women have little interest in sports.

3. Men say that women change the subject when they're losing an argument.

4. According to men, women talk too much.

---

accuse A of ~ A를 ~로 비난하다, 고소하다 **argument** 말다툼, 논쟁; 주장

The implied main idea is:

a. Men think women don't trust them.

b. Men have various complaints about women.

c. Men accuse women of talking too much.

d. Men have strong positive and negative views about women.

Explanations

a. too narrow to be the implied main idea: 단지 한 가지 진술에만 포함되는 너무 세부적 내용이다.

b. "여자들에 대한 남자들의 불평, 불만"을 포괄적으로 말하고 있다. 네 가지 각각의 진술들은 모두 이러한 불평에 관한 것들이다. 그래서 항목 b가 네 가지 모든 진술들을 모두 포괄하는 요지이다.

c. too narrow to be the main idea.

d. too broad.

PRACTICE 1

Group 1: 아래 세부적 진술들을 모두 포괄하는 요지를 고르시오.

1. Laser beams are used to guide bombs to their targets.

2. The communications industry uses lasers to carry pictures and voices through cables.

3. Medical uses of lasers include the removal of birthmarks and the unclogging of arteries.

4. Businesses use lasers to read bar codes and to guide robots through production-line tasks.

bomb 폭탄 removal 제거 birthmark 모반 unclogging 뚫기 artery 동맥

The implied main idea is:

a. Laser beams are the best source of energy.

b. Lasers now have only limited use compared with what they will do in the future.

c. Lasers are used by the military.

d. Lasers are used in a variety of ways.

Hint: The first four sentences discuss a variety of uses for lasers.

Group 2: 아래 세부적 진술들을 모두 포괄하는 요지를 고르시오.

1. Smoking is a major contribution to heart disease.

2. High cholesterol due to poor diet is a major cause of heart disease.

3. High blood pressure can cause heart disease.

4. Recently it was discovered that inactivity can damage the heart.

contribution 기여, 공헌
contribute to ~에 기여(공헌)하다 **due to** ~ 때문에 **inactivity** 무활동, 운동부족 **factor** 요인

The implied main idea is:

a. Heart disease is the number one killer of Americans.

b. Various factors can contribute to heart disease.

c. Only four factors contribute to heart disease.

d. People who exercise, don't smoke, and eat well will not get heart disease.

Group 3: 아래 세부적 진술들을 모두 포괄하는 요지를 고르시오.

1. An octopus may escape its enemies by shooting out a jet of water that gives it a burst of speed.

2. The octopus can avoid being discovered by changing its body color so that it blends into the environment.

3. The octopus can also avoid attack by releasing its ink, which confuses attackers.

4. The released ink also dulls an attacker's sense of smell, making it harder to find the octopus.

escape 탈출하다 **a jet of water** 물 분사 **a burst of speed** 폭발적인 속도
blend into the environment 주변 환경에 섞이게 되다, 녹아들어가다 **dull** 무디게 하다

The implied main idea is:

a. An octopus must protect itself from enemies.

b. An octopus has several means of defense.

c. An octopus has an interesting lifestyle.

d. An octopus can change its coloring and blend into the environment.

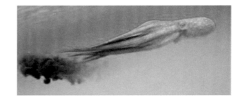

Group 4: 아래 세부적 진술들을 모두 포괄하는 요지를 고르시오.

1. Egypt's pyramids are the oldest existing buildings in the world. These ancient tombs are also among the world's largest structures.

2. The largest pyramid stands taller than a 40-story building and covers an area greater than that of ten football fields.

3. More than 80 pyramids still exist, and their once-smooth limestone surfaces hide secret passageways and rooms.

4. The pyramids of ancient Egypt served a vital purpose: to protect the pharaohs' bodies after death.

5. Each pyramid held not only the pharaoh's preserved body but also all the goods he would need in his life after death.

— Adapted from Sporre, *The Creative Impulse*, 6th ed., p.45.

existing 현존하는 **once-smooth limestone** 한때 매끄러운 석회암
passageway 통로 **hold** 소장하다, 보관하다 **preserved** 보존된 **contents** 내용물

The implied main idea is:

a. Pyramids are large, ancient buildings.

b. Pyramids are massive structures, whose contents reflect the ancient Egyptians' beliefs.

c. Pyramids are tombs that were built for the pharaohs.

d. Pyramids are remarkable.

STEP 4. 문단내에 암시된 요지(Implied Main Idea) 찾기

4 번째 단계에서는 문단속에 언급되어 있지 않은 요지를 찾아내는 연습이다. 문단에 숨어 있는 요지를 찾기 위해서는 다음 3 가지 질문을 반드시 기억하라.

1st Q: **What is the paragraph about?** → *Topic*

2nd Q: **What is the main point the author trying to make about the topic?**
→ *Main Idea*

3rd Q: **Does all or most material in the paragraph support this Main Idea?**

Example: 아래 문단을 읽고 이 글에 내포되어 있는 요지를 고르시오.

   If people stop to think about the plots in children's stories, they may be surprised. *Hansel and Gretel*, for example, were abandoned by their father and stepmother and left to wander in a dark forest. *Cinderella* was treated like a slave by her stepmother and stepsisters. *Little Red Riding Hood* was eaten by a wild animal, and the three blind mice had their tails cut off by the farmer's wife.

The implied main idea is:

a. Cinderella was treated like a slave.

b. Children's stories are about stepfamilies.

c. Children's stories often deal with evil and violence.

d. Animals and children are important characters in children's stories.

 Explanations

이 문단의 요지에 대한 중요한 단서는 첫 문장에 있다. 첫 문장에 있는 'plots in children's stories'가 문단의 topic이다. 나머지 문장들은 3개의 예시를 들면서 어린이 동화의 내용들이 모두 폭력적인 것으로 묘사한다. 그래서 'children's stories'에 대해 필자가 말하고자 하는 요지는 "어린이 동화들은 종종 악과 폭력성을 다룬다"가 가장 적합하다.

a & b: too narrow to be the main idea.
c: 어린이 동화들이 악함과 폭력적인 행위를 다루고 있다는 것은 사람들을 놀라게 하는 사실이다. 문단의 모든 예문들은 악함과 폭력적인 내용을 담고 있는 어린이 동화들에 관한 것이다. 따라서 c가 이 문단의 숨은 요지를 나타낸다.
d: 어린이 동화의 폭력싱과는 아무런 관련이 없다.

PRACTICE 2

아래 문단을 읽고 이 글에 내포되어 있는 요지를 고르시오.

1.   Why do some people avoid crossing the path of a black cat? The reason is centuries old. People in the Middle Ages believed that witches were very dangerous creatures who could change themselves into black cats. Witches were also thought to be easily upset. So, if you wanted to avoid trouble, the safest thing to do was simply avoid all black cats.

witch 마녀 **creature** 창조물, 피조물; 생물 **superstition** 미신

The implied main idea is:

a.   Some people avoid crossing the path of a black cat.

b.   Superstitions have interesting historical backgrounds.

c.   The fear of crossing the path of a black cat comes from beliefs about witches in the Middle Ages.

d.   During the Middle Ages, people believed that witches were dangerous and could change themselves into black cats.

2.   Two workers on the twentieth floor of a building saw a bird banging its head against the outside of their office window. They rescued the bird and took it to a nearby animal hospital. The vet explained that what had happened was not unusual. The bird had eaten berries which had been on the vine long enough to ferment. The sugar had partially turned to alcohol. The bird, in other words, was drunk. The vet gave it time to sober up and then released it.

---

vet (veterinarian) 수의사 **ferment** 발효하다 **partially** 부분적으로 **sober up** 술에서 깨어나다, 정신이 들다

The implied main idea is:

a. Two office workers learned that birds could get drunk.

b. Workers in skyscrapers often rescue birds.

c. Birds like to bang their heads against windows.

d. A drunken bird should be taken to an animal hospital.

3.   Before the twentieth century, millions of people died needlessly in hospitals. Back then, doctors didn't wash their hands between tasks. Little was known about germs and how they were spread. Doctors would finish one operation, then immediately start on another operation. Then they would examine patients, never realizing that they were carrying bacteria from one person to another. In many cases, they seriously infected the very people they were trying to cure.

---

needlessly 불필요하게 **germ** 세균 **operation** 수술 **infect** 감염시키다 **unknowingly** 모르고

The implied main idea is:

a.   Before the twentieth century, doctors knew very little about disease.

b.   Before much was known about germs, doctors unknowingly cause much illness and death by spreading germs.

c.   Before the twentieth century, doctors would finish one operation and go on to another without washing their hands.

d.   When little was known about germs, people's cleanliness habits were poor.

4.   The Roman emperor Nero was probably behind some of the earliest frozen desserts. He had snow brought to him from nearby mountains to cool his wine cellar. Historians believe that the snow was also mixed with fruit juices and honey. It wasn't until the 1200s, however, that the first frozen dessert made with milk reached Europe. It was introduced by Marco Polo, who brought the recipe from the Orient.

It was not until ~ that S+V... ~해서야 비로소...했다

The implied main idea is:

a. There are many delicious and healthful frozen desserts.

b. Some of the earliest known frozen desserts were made for Nero.

c. The history of frozen desserts was influenced by Nero and Marco Polo.

d. A frozen dessert in ancient Rome consisted of snow, fruit, juices, and honey.

5.   Some workers skip breakfast and try to make up for it by eating a big lunch. Studies show that workers who do this lose as much efficiency at work as people who've missed a whole night's sleep. Workers who eat a high-protein breakfast and a light lunch, on the other hand, tend to be energetic and efficient throughout the day. Furthermore, a separate study proved that teens who eat breakfast do far better in school than their classmates who don't.

---

make up for 보충하다, 만회하다 **efficiency** 효율(성), 능률 **efficient** 효율적인 **high-protein** 고단백질

The implied main idea is:

   a. Eating a good breakfast increases one's efficiency throughout the day.

   b. Skipping lunch probably does not make one less efficient.

   c. Teens who want to do well in school should eat a good breakfast.

   d. A glass of milk, whole wheat bread, and cheese make a good breakfast.

STEP 5. 암시된 요지(Implied Main Idea)를 직접 쓰기

5번째 단계는 문단속에 언급되지 않은 요지를 파악해서 직접 쓰는 마지막 훈련단계이다. 문단에 숨어 있는 요지를 찾기 위해서는 이전 단계와 마찬가지로 다음과 같은 절차를 거쳐야 한다.

---

1. First look for the topic.

2. Then decide on what the author is saying about the topic.

3. State this idea in your own words.

Example: 아래 문단의 Topic을 적고 주어진 단어를 사용하여 문단의 요지문을 완성하시오. (어형 변화 필요)

The factor most often named by workers as being important to <u>job satisfaction</u> is a feeling of accomplishment. The opportunity for advancement is the next most popular factor. Close behind that is pay. Next come job security and shorter hours at work.

Topic: _____

Implied main idea:

There are several _____ that workers feel are most _____

_____ at work.   (contribute/ satisfaction/ to/ factors)

요지: 근로자들이 직장 만족도에 가장 크게 기여한다고 생각하는 몇 가지 요인들이 있다.

 Explanations

이 글의 Topic은 직장인이 생각하는 '직업 만족도'(Job satisfaction)의 요인들이다. 가장 중요한 요인으로는 첫 번째로 성취감(Feeling of accomplishment)이고 다음으로는 승진의 기회(Opportunity for advancement)이며 바로 그 다음이 급여(Pay)이고 다음이 직장의 안정성(Job security)과 짧은 근무 시간(Shorter hours at work)이다. 글의 요지는 "There are several <u>factors</u> that workers feel are most <u>contributing to satisfaction</u> at work."이다.

Training 적용 훈련 문제

아래 각 문단을 읽고 문단의 Topic과 암시된 요지를 적어라. 괄호안에 주어진 어휘를 사용해서 빈칸을 완성하라. (필요시 어형 변화 가능)

1.

I was in an alley dressed in light summer clothing. Coming out of the darkness at the end of the alley were <u>hundreds of large gray rats</u>. Their razor-sharp teeth glistened with saliva, and their eyes glowed red with a cold fury. I turned to run away, but attacking in the other direction were a <u>dozen angry dogs</u> – pit bulls! And these particular pit bulls were foaming at the mouth; <u>they all had rabies</u>. "Just my luck," I muttered and <u>did my best to wake up as quickly as possible</u>.

alley 골목길 glisten 반짝이다 saliva 침, 타액 glow 빛나다 fury 분노, 격분 rabies 광견병 mutter 중얼거리다

1. 이 글의 Topic은? _____

2. 주어진 단어를 사용하여 이 글의 요지(Implied Main Idea)를 완성하시오.

I _____.

(really/ a/ had/ dream/ frightening)

요지: 나는 정말 무서운 꿈을 꿨다

2.

A team of researchers conducted a <u>survey on patients</u> who had suffered serious illnesses. Sixty of the patients had suffered a heart attack, while another thirty were breast cancer patients. All had completed therapy for their medical conditions at the time of the survey. Subjects were asked what <u>positive changes</u> had happened to them after their illness. About half of the participants reported <u>healthy lifestyle changes</u>. And over a quarter reported <u>a greater appreciation of life and health, along with improved close relationships</u>. Other common <u>positive changes</u> included feeling lucky to be given a second chance and a better understanding of others.

---

heart attack 심장마비 **therapy** 치료 **subject** 실험대상자 **participant** 참가자 **appreciation** 감사

---

1. 이 글의 Topic은? _____

2. 괄호 안에 주어진 단어를 사용하여 이 글의 요지(Implied Main Idea)를 완성하시오.

A survey of patients shows that _____

_____.

(positive/ can/ serious illness/ have/ effects/ their illness/ after)

요지: 환자를 대상으로 한 설문 조사에 따르면 심각한 질병은 질병후에 긍정적인 영향을 미칠 수 있다

3. 괄호 안에 주어진 단어를 사용하여 이 글의 요지를 다르게 표현(Paraphrasing)하시오.

A survey of patients shows that many individuals _____

_____ in their lives.

(positive changes/ serious illness/ have suffered/ who/ experience)

요지: 환자들을 대상으로 실시한 조사에 따르면, <u>심각한 질병을 앓았던</u> 많은 사람들은 생활에서 <u>긍정적인 변화를 경험한다</u>.

 **Explanations**

이 글의 Topic은 "A survey of patients"이고, 환자에 대한 설문조사의 결과들을 요약(Summary)하면 요지가 된다. 즉, "A survey of patients shows that <u>serious illness can have positive effects after their illness.</u>"가 이 문단의 요지가 될 수 있다.

3.

Very young infants enjoy big, bright toys to look at and chew. Colorful mobiles, squeaky animals, and strings of hard rubber beads are good choices for them. Older babies who can sit up enjoy toys they can grasp and explore with their hands. Cloth picture books, cups that nest inside each other, and balls covered with textured fabric will please a child of this age. Children between the ages of eighteen months and three years like toys matched to their increasing freedom of movement. Toy shopping carts, lawn mowers, wagons, and other push-and-pull toys are popular with children of this age.

squeaky 삑삑 소리나는 string 줄 bead 구슬 grasp (손으로)잡다
nest inside ~안에 둥지를 틀다 textured fabric 질감 직물 matched to ~에(와) 잘 맞는, 잘 어울리는

1. 이 글의 Topic은? _____

2. 괄호 안에 주어진 단어를 사용하여 이 글의 요지(Implied Main Idea)를 완성하시오.

At different _____, children like _____.

(specific/ development/ kinds of toys/ stages)

요지: 다양한 발달 단계에서 아이들은 특정 종류의 장난감을 좋아한다.

3. 괄호 안에 주어진 단어를 사용하여 이 글의 요지를 다르게 표현(Paraphrasing)하시오.

Children's toy _____ are _____

_____.

(their developmental/ preferences/ stages/ influenced by)

요지: 아이들의 장난감 선호도는 발달 단계에 영향을 받는다.

4.

One odd suggestion for curing hiccups is to cut some holes in a paper bag, put the bag over your head, and breathe deeply. Another is to put a teaspoon of sugar on your tongue; by the time the sugar has disappeared, some claim, so have the hiccups. Some people feel that the way to get rid of hiccups is to cover a glass of water with a clean handkerchief and then drink the water through the hankie. If none of these methods works, you might try yet another odd cure for hiccups: stand on your head, close your eyes tightly, take a deep breath, and recite "Mary Had a Little Lamb."

odd 이상한 claim 주장하다 get rid of; remove 제거하다, 없애다
handkerchief 손수건 work 효과가 있다 stand on one's head 물구나무서다 recite 암송하다

1. 이 글의 Topic은? _____

2. 괄호 안에 주어진 단어를 사용하여 이 글의 요지(Implied Main Idea)를 완성하시오.

There are _____ for _____.

(curing/ remedies/ hiccups/ some odd)

요지: 딸꾹질을 치료하는 몇 가지 이상한 치료법이 있다.

3. 괄호 안에 주어진 단어를 사용하여 이 글의 요지를 다르게 표현(Paraphrasing)하시오.

Various _____ are suggested as _____

_____.

(potential cures/ unconventional methods/ for hiccups)

요지: 딸꾹질에 대한 잠재적인 치료법으로 다양한 비전통적인 방법이 제안된다.

5.

Polynesians once believed that a total eclipse of the sun occurred when the sun and moon made love. The stars were the offspring. Some North American Indian tribes believed that an eclipse signaled the death of a celestial body. Other tribes believed that coyotes that roamed the stars hunted during an eclipse. In China eclipses were so significant that three thousand years ago, two astronomers who failed to predict an eclipse were beheaded.

---

total eclipse 개기일식 offspring 자손, 새끼 celestial body 천체 roam 배회하다, 돌아다니다 astronomer 천문학자 fail to do ~하지 못하다 be beheaded 참수형을 당하다

---

1. 이 글의 Topic은? _____

2. 괄호 안에 주어진 단어를 사용하여 이 글의 요지(Implied Main Idea)를 완성하시오.

_____ are _____ to many _____.

(culturally/ societies/ significant/ eclipses)

요지: 일식은 많은 사회에서 문화적으로 중요하다.

3. 괄호 안에 주어진 단어를 사용하여 이 글의 요지를 다르게 표현(Paraphrasing)하시오.

Eclipses are _____ and have _____

across _____.

(different societies and civilizations/ varied interpretations/ culturally significant)

요지: 일식은 문화적으로 중요하며 다양한 사회와 문명에 걸쳐 다양한 해석을 가지고 있다.

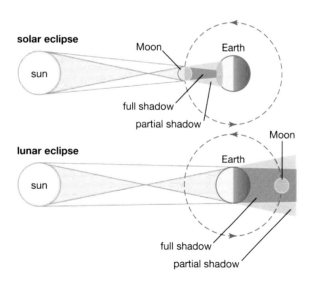

6.

Chocolate causes pimples. If you are bitten by a snake, you should suck the snakebite to prevent poisoning from the venom. If you have an ulcer, you should drink milk. What do all of these common medical beliefs have in common? They are all false. Breakouts of pimples are linked with an increase in the body's production of a certain hormone, and there may be a genetic link as well. The bacteria present in your mouth will increase the risk of infecting a snakebite wound. Milk contains lactic acid, which stimulates the acid in the stomach and causes an ulcer to become irritated.

pimple 여드름(acne) poisoning 중독 venom 독 ulcer (위)궤양 breakout (피부) 발진, 발생 genetic 유전적인 present in ~에 존재하는 lactic acid 유산, 젖산 stimulate 자극하다 irritate 염증을 일으키게 하다

---

1. 이 글의 Topic은? _____

2. 괄호 안에 주어진 단어를 사용하여 이 글의 요지(Implied Main Idea)를 완성하시오.

   Many _____ are _____.

   (misconceptions or falsehoods/ beliefs/ medical/ common)

   요지: 많은 일반적인 의학적 믿음은 오해 또는 거짓입니다.

3. 괄호 안에 주어진 단어를 사용하여 이 글의 요지를 다르게 표현(Paraphrasing)하시오.

   _____, such as chocolate causing pimples, sucking

   snakebites to prevent poisoning, and drinking milk for ulcers, _____.

   (are/ Common medical beliefs/ false)

   요지: 초콜릿이 여드름을 유발한다는 것, 중독을 막기 위해 뱀에 물린 곳을 빠는 것, 그리고 위궤양이 생기면 우유를 마신다는 것과 같은 일반적인 의학적 믿음은 잘못된 것이다.

7.

When you're sick, remember to drink plenty of fluids to keep from becoming dehydrated. Also eat small, frequent meals. Small meals may tire you out less and minimize stomach problems. Also useful is a low-fat diet, which is easier on your digestive system. A low-fat diet may also increase the activity of your body' cells that fight illness. A final dietary guideline for when you're sick is to drink a fruit smoothie when you're hungry. Smoothies are easy to swallow and digest and full of healing vitamins and minerals. They are also easy to make — just throw strawberries, bananas, orange juice, plain yogurt, a pinch of wheat germ and some ice into a blender.

fluid 수분, 체액; 유동성의 **dehydrate** 탈수시키다 **digestive system** 소화 시스템
dietary guideline 식이요법 지침 **a pinch of** ~약간의, 소량의 **wheat germ** 밀 배아, 밀 맥아

---

1. 이 글의 Topic은? _____

2. 괄호 안에 주어진 단어를 사용하여 이 글의 요지(Implied Main Idea)를 완성하시오.

Certain _____ can help you _____.

(recover/ an illness/ from/ dietary guidelines)

요지: 특정 식이 지침은 질병에서 회복하는 데 도움이 될 수 있다.

3. 괄호 안에 주어진 단어를 사용하여 이 글의 요지를 다르게 표현(Paraphrasing)하시오.

Certain dietary guidelines can be _____ in _____
and _____ during illness.

(minimizing discomfort/ promoting recovery/ beneficial)

요지: 특정 식이 지침은 회복을 촉진하고 질병 중 불편함을 최소화하는 데 도움이 될 수 있다.

Challenge 1등급 도전

아래 지문을 읽고 물음에 답하시오.

1.

Hydroelectric power is a clean and renewable power source. However, there are a few things about dams that are important to know. To build a hydroelectric dam, a large area must be flooded behind the dam. Whole communities sometimes have to be moved to another place. Entire forests can be drowned. The water released from the dam can be colder than usual and this can affect the ecosystems in the rivers downstream. It can also wash away riverbanks and destroy life on the river bottoms. The worst effect of dams has been observed on salmon that have to travel upstream to lay their eggs. If blocked by a dam, the salmon life cycle cannot be completed. [고 1 모의]

— Adapted from Sheri Amsel, *The Everything Kids' Environment Book*, 2007

*hydroelectric: 수력 발전의 **ecosystem: 생태계

---

1. 다음 글의 주제로 가장 적절한 것은?

① necessity of saving energy

② dark sides of hydroelectric dams

③ types of hydroelectric power plants

④ popularity of renewable power sources

⑤ importance of protecting the environment

2. 이 글의 요지로 적절하지 않은 것은?

a. While hydroelectric power is a clean and renewable energy source, the construction and operation of hydroelectric dams have significant environmental drawbacks.

b. Hydroelectric power, despite being a clean and renewable energy source, poses significant environmental side-effects.

c. Hydroelectric power is an ideal and flawless energy solution with no adverse effects on the environment, offering sustainability without any drawbacks.

 *Explanations*

[해석]

수력 발전은 깨끗하고 재생 가능한 에너지원이다. 하지만 알아두는 것이 중요한 댐에 관한 몇 가지가 있다. 수력발전 댐을 건설하기 위해서, 댐 뒤의 넓은 지역이 반드시 물에 잠기게 된다. 때때로 지역 사회 전체가 다른 지역으로 이주되어야 한다. 숲 전체가 물에 잠길 수도 있다. 댐에서 방류된 물은 평소보다 더 차서 이것이 하류의 강 생태계에 영향을 미칠 수 있다. 그것은 또한 강기슭을 유실되게 하고 강바닥의 생물을 파괴할 수도 있다. 댐의 가장 나쁜 영향은 알을 낳기 위해 흐름을 거슬러 올라가야 하는 연어에서 관찰되어 왔다. 댐으로 막히면, 연어의 라이프 사이클은 완결될 수 없다.

[해설]

1..이 글의 요지는 " There are a few bad tings about hydroelectric dams" 가 될 수 있다. 그러므로 "dark sides of hydroelectric dams" 이 글의 주제로 가장 적절하다.

① 에너지 절약의 필요성 　② 수력 발전 댐의 어두운 면 　③ 수력 발전소의 유형

④ 재생 가능한 에너지원의 인기 　⑤ 환경 보호의 중요성

2. 이 글의 요지로 적합한 것은 a 와 b 이고, c 는 적합하지 않다.

a. 수력 발전은 깨끗하고 재생 가능한 에너지원이지만 수력 발전 댐의 건설 및 운영에는 심각한 환경적 단점이 있다.

b. 수력 발전은 깨끗하고 재생 가능한 에너지원임에도 불구하고 심각한 환경 부작용을 초래한다.

c. 수력 발전은 환경에 악영향을 미치지 않는 이상적이고 완벽한 에너지 솔루션으로 단점 없이 지속가능성을 제공한다.

[어휘]

renewable power source 재생가능한 에너지원(전력원) **be flooded** 물에 잠기다, 범람되다 **be drowned** (물에) 잠기다, 침수되다; 익사하다 **release** 방류[방출]하다 **downstream** 하류의, 하류에 **wash away** ~을 유실되게 하다 **riverbank** 강기슭, 강둑 **upstream** 흐름을 거슬러 올라가, 상류로 **lay** (알)을 낳다 **necessity** 필요성 **drawback** 단점 **pose** ~을 초래하다 **side effect** 부작용 **adverse effect** 부작용, 역효과, 악영향 **sustainability** 지속가능성

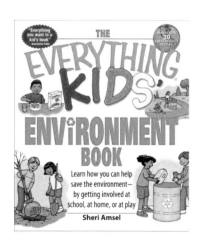

2.

When it comes to climate change, many blame the fossil fuel industry for pumping greenhouse gases, the agricultural sector for burning rainforests, or the fashion industry for producing excessive clothes. But wait, what drives these industrial activities? Our consumption. Climate change is a summed product of each person's behavior. For example, the fossil fuel industry is a popular scapegoat in the climate crisis. But why do they drill and burn fossil fuels? We provide them strong financial incentives: some people regularly travel on airplanes and cars that burn fossil fuels. Some people waste electricity generated by burning fuel in power plants. Some people use and throw away plastic products derived from crude oil every day. Blaming the fossil fuel industry while engaging in these behaviors is a slap in our own face.[고1모의]

*scapegoat 희생양

1. 이 글의 요지로 가장 적절한 것은?

   a. The blame on the fossil fuel industry for climate change is misplaced, and individual consumer behavior is a significant contributing factor.

   b. The agricultural sector and the fashion industry are the root causes in climate change.

   c. The financial incentives provided to the fossil fuel industry are the primary driver of climate change.

2. 다음 글의 제목으로 가장 적절한 것은?

   a. Consumer Behavior: The Driving Force Behind Climate Change

   b. The Scapegoat Syndrome: Misplaced Blame in the Climate Crisis

   c. From Consumption to Crisis: Understanding Climate Change Dynamics

3. 밑줄 친 a slap in our own face 가 의미하는 바는 무엇인가? (한글로 적으시오)

 *Explanations*

[해석]

기후 변화에 관해 많은 사람들은 온실가스를 배출하는 것에 대해 화석 연료 산업을, 열대 우림을 태우는 것에 대해 농업 분야를, 혹은 과다한 의복을 생산하는 것에 대해 패션 산업을 탓한다. 하지만 잠깐만, 무엇이 이러한 산업 활동들을 가동시키는가? 우리의 소비이다. 기후 변화는 각 개인 행위의 합쳐진 산물이다. 예를 들어 화석 연료 산업은 기후 위기에 있어서 일반적인 희생양이다. 하지만 왜 그들은 화석 연료를 시추하고 태울까? 우리가 그들에게 강력한 금전적인 동기를 제공한다. 예를 들어, 어떤 사람들은 화석 연료를 태우는 비행기와 차로 정기적으로 여행한다. 어떤 사람들은 발전소에서 연료를 태움으로써 생산된 전기를 낭비한다. 어떤 사람들은 원유로부터 얻어진 플라스틱 제품을 매일 사용하고 버린다. 이러한 행위들에 참여하면서 화석 연료 산업을 탓하는 것은 <u>스스로의 얼굴 때리기</u>이다.

[해설]

이 글 전체 내용을 요약하면 "화석 연료, 농업 및 패션 부문과 같은 다양한 산업이 종종 기후 변화의 원인으로 지목되지만, **근본 원인은 개별 소비자 행동에 있다**. 왜냐하면 이러한 산업들은 과도한 여행, 에너지 낭비 및 일회용 플라스틱 사용과 같은 활동으로 인한 강력한 재정적 인센티브에 반응하기 때문이다."이다.

Summary: While various industries, such as the fossil fuel, agricultural, and fashion sectors, are often blamed for climate change, <u>the root cause lies in individual consumer behavior</u>, as these industries respond to strong financial incentives driven by activities such as excessive travel, energy waste, and disposable plastic use.

1. 글의 요지는 **a.** "The blame on the fossil fuel industry for climate change is misplaced, and individual consumer behavior is a significant contributing factor. (기후 변화에 대한 화석 연료 산업의 책임은 잘못된 것이며, 개별 소비자 행동이 중요한 기여 요인이다)" 가 적절하다.

2. 글의 제목으로는 **a.** "소비자 행동: 기후 변화의 원동력(Consumer Behavior: The Driving Force Behind Climate Change)"이 가장 적절하다.

3. 밑줄 <u>a slap in our own face</u> 가 궁극적으로 의미하는 바는 "기후 변화에대한 우리의 책임을 인식하지 못하는 것"(failing to recognize our responsibility for climate change)이다.

[어휘]

When it comes to ~에 관한한 **fossil fuel** 화석 연료 **excessive** 과도한 **drive** ~을 이끌다, 유발하다 **consumption** 소비 **summed product** 합산된 산물 **scapegoat** 희생양 **drill** (석유를) 시추하다 **financial** 금전적인, 금융의, 재정적인 **incentive** 인센티브; 동기유발 **derived from** ~로부터 나온(얻어진), ~로부터 비롯된 **crude oil** (석유) 원유 **engage in** ~에 관여(참여)하다 **a slap in one's own face** 자기 자신의 뺨 때리기 **misplaced** 잘못된, 잘못 짚은 **contributing factor** 기여하는 요인 **root cause** 근본 원인 **primary driver** 주요한 유발자 **driving force** 원동력

3.

Many people look for safety and security in popular thinking. They figure that if a lot of people are doing something, then it must be right. It must be a good idea. If most people accept it, then it probably represents fairness, equality, compassion, and sensitivity, right? Not necessarily. Popular thinking said the earth was the center of the universe, yet Copernicus studied the stars and planets and proved mathematically that the earth and the other planets in our solar system revolved around the sun. Popular thinking said surgery didn't require clean instruments, yet Joseph Lister studied the high death rates in hospitals and introduced antiseptic practices that immediately saved lives. Popular thinking said that women shouldn't have the right to vote, yet people like Emmeline Pankhurst and Susan B. Anthony fought for and won that right. We must always remember _____. People may say that there's safety in numbers, but that's not always true.[고2모의]

— Adapted from John C. Maxwell, *How Successful People Think: Change Your Thinking, Change Your Life*, 2014, p.163

*antiseptic: 멸균의

---

1. 다음 빈칸에 들어갈 말로 가장 적절한 것을 고르시오.

① majority rule should be founded on fairness

② the crowd is generally going in the right direction

③ the roles of leaders and followers can change at any time

④ people behave in a different fashion to others around them

⑤ there is a huge difference between acceptance and intelligence

2. 괄호 안에 주어진 단어를 사용하여 이 글의 요지문을 완성하시오.

Despite the inclination to find safety and security in popular thinking, historical examples demonstrate the importance of _____ _____, revealing that _____ does not necessarily _____.

(equal/ questioning/ widespread/ conventional/ acceptance/ intelligence/ wisdom)

요약: 대중적인 생각에서 안전과 안심을 찾으려는 경향에도 불구하고, 역사적 사례는 통념에 의문을 제기하는 것의 중요성을 증명해주며, 널리 받아들여지는 것(대중적인 수용)이 반드시 지성과 같지는 않다는 것을 보여준다.

Explanations

[해석]

많은 사람이 대중적인 사고에서 안전과 안심을 찾는다. 그들은 만약 많은 사람이 무언가를 하고 있다면, 그것은 틀림없이 옳을 것으로 생각한다. 그것은 좋은 생각임이 틀림없다. 만약 대부분의 사람들이 그것을 받아들인다면, 그것은 아마도 공정함, 평등함, 동정심, 그리고 민감성을 상징할 것이다, 그러한가? 꼭 그렇다고 할 수는 없다. 대중적인 사고는 지구가 우주의 중심이라고 했지만, Copernicus 는 별과 행성을 연구했고 지구와 태양계의 다른 행성들이 태양 주위를 돈다는 것을 수학적으로 증명했다. 대중적인 사고는 수술이 깨끗한 도구를 필요로 하지 않는다고 말했지만, Joseph Lister 는 병원에서의 높은 사망률을 연구했고 즉시 생명을 구하는 멸균법을 도입했다. 대중적인 사고는 여성들이 투표권을 가져서는 안 된다고 했지만, Emmeline Pankhurst 와 Susan B. Anthony 같은 사람들은 그 권리를 위해 싸웠고 쟁취했다. 우리는 항상 **수용과 지성 사이에 큰 차이가 있다는 것**을 기억해야 한다. 사람들은 수가 많은 편이 더 안전하다고 말할지도 모르지만, 그것이 항상 사실인 것은 아니다.

[해설]

1. 빈칸 추론: "대중적인 사고에서 안전과 안심을 찾지만 반드시 옳다고 할 수는 없다. 대중적인 사고가 옳지 않다는 예들로, 지동설이 증명되었고, 수술의 멸균법이 도입되었고, 여성들의 투표권이 쟁취되었다. 그러므로 **수용(=대중적 사고)과 지성(=옳은 것) 사이에 큰 차이가 있다**"라는 것을 기억해야한다" 라는 주장이 이 글 전체의 맥락이다. 그러므로 빈칸 정답은 ⑤이다.

2. 이 글의 요약문은 다음과 같다:

Despite the inclination to find safety and security in popular thinking, historical examples demonstrate the importance of <u>questioning conventional wisdom</u>, revealing that <u>widespread acceptance</u> does not necessarily <u>equal intelligence</u>.

[어휘]

security 안심, 안전; 보안, 안보 **popular thinking** 대중적 사고 **figure** 생각하다 **represent** 나타내다, 상징하다; 대표하다 **fairness** 공정성 **equality** 평등 **compassion** 공감; 동정심; 연민 **sensitivity** 감수성, 민감성 **Not necessarily** 반드시 ~인 것은 아니다 **revolve** 회전하다 **surgery** 수술; 외과 **the right to vote** 투표할 권리 **majority rule** 다수결의 원칙 **be founded on** ~에 기초(근거)가 되다 **fashion** 방식, 방법 **instrument** 도구, 기기; 악기 **despite** ~임에도 불구하고 **inclination** 경향, 추세, 성향 **demonstrate** 보여주다, 시연하다, 입증하다 **question** ~에 의문을 제기하다 **conventional wisdom** 사회적(일반) 통념 **equal** ~와 같다, 동일하다 **intelligence** 지성, 지능

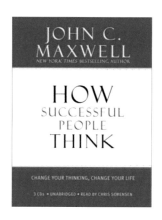

4.

Even those with average talent can produce notable work in the various sciences, so long as they do not try to embrace all of them at once. Instead, they should concentrate attention on one subject after another (that is, in different periods of time), although later work will weaken earlier attainments in the other spheres. This amounts to saying that the brain adapts to universal science in *time* but not in *space*. In fact, even those with great abilities proceed in this way. Thus, when we are astonished by someone with publications in different scientific fields, realize that each topic was explored during a specific period of time. Knowledge gained earlier certainly will not have disappeared from the mind of the author, but it will have become simplified by condensing into formulas or greatly abbreviated symbols. Thus, sufficient space remains for the perception and learning of new images on the cerebral blackboard. — Adapted from Santiago Ramon Y Cajal, *Advice for a Young Investigator*, 2004,p. 25

*condense 응축하다 ****cerebral** 대뇌의

1. 이 글을 한 문장으로 요약하고자 한다. 빈칸에 들어갈 말로 가장 적절한 것은? [24 수능]

Exploring one scientific subject after another _____(A)_____ remarkable work across the sciences, as the previously gained knowledge is retained in simplified forms within the brain, which _____(B)_____ room for new learning.

	(A)	(B)
①	enables	leaves
②	challenges	spares
③	delays	creates
④	requires	removes
⑤	invites	diminishes

2. 위 글의 요지문이다. 빈칸에 알맞은 단어를 넣어 요지문을 완성하시오.

Individuals, regardless of talent level, can a_____ notable success in various sciences by focusing on one subject at a time over different periods, as the brain adapts to universal science over time, allowing for the retention of earlier knowledge in simplified forms and c_____ space for the acquisition of new information.

Explanations

[해석]

평균적인 재능을 가진 사람이라도 다양한 과학 분야에서 주목할 만한 성과를 낼 수 있는데, 한 번에 그것들 모두를 수용하려고 하지 않는 한 그렇다. 대신에 그들은 한 주제 다음에 다른 주제로 (즉, 다른 기간에) 집중해야 하는데, 비록 나중의 작업은 다른 영역에서의 더 이전의 성취를 약화시킬 수 있지만 말이다. 이것은 뇌가 보편적인 과학에 '*시간*'속에서 적응하는 것이지 '*공간*'속에서 적응하는 것이 아니라고 말하는 것과 마찬가지이다. 사실, 뛰어난 능력을 가진 사람들도 이런 식으로 나아간다. 따라서, 우리가 서로 다른 과학 분야에 출판물을 가진 사람에게 놀랄 때, 각 주제가 특정 기간 동안 탐구되었다는 것을 인식하라. 더 이전에 얻은 지식은 확실히 저자의 마음에서 사라지지 않았을 것이지만 그것은 공식이나 크게 축약된 기호로 응축되어 단순화되었을 것이다. 따라서 대뇌 칠판에 새로운 이미지를 인식하고 학습할 수 있는 충분한 공간이 남아 있다.

요약문: 하나의 과학 주제를 탐구한 다음에 다른 주제를 탐구하는 것은 과학 전반에 걸친 주목할 만한 작업을 **가능하게 하는데**, 이전에 습득된 지식은 뇌 안에서 단순화된 형태로 유지되며 이는 새로운 학습을 위한 공간을 **남겨두기** 때문이다.

[해설]

1. 과학 주제를 차례로 탐구하게 되면 이전에 습득한 지식은 저자의 마음에서 사라지지 않고 공식이나 크게 축약된 기호로 응축되어 단순화되어 새로운 이미지를 인식하고 학습할 수 있는 공간이 충분히 남아 있어 과학 전반에 걸쳐 주목할 만한 연구를 할 수 있다는 내용의 글이다. 따라서 요약문의 빈칸 (A), (B)에 들어갈 말로 가장 적절한 것은 ① '가능하게 하다 - 남겨두다'이다. ② 어렵게 하다 – 남겨놓다 ③ 지연시키다 . 만들다 ④ 필요로 하다 – 없애다 ⑤ 가져오다 – 감소시키다

2. 빈칸 정답은 **achieve** 와 **creating** 이고 요지문 해석은 다음과 같다:

재능 수준에 관계없이 개인은 여러 기간에 걸쳐 한 번에 하나의 주제에 집중함으로써 다양한 과학 분야에서 주목할만한 성공을 **거둘 수 있**습니다. 왜냐하면 뇌는 시간이 지남에 따라 보편적 과학에 적응하여 이전 지식을 단순화된 형태로 유지하고 새로운 정보를 습득할 수 있는 공간을 **만들기** 때문입니다.

[어휘]

notable 주목할 만한 **as long as S+V** ~하는 한 **embrace** 수용(포용)하다, 받아들이다, 포옹하다, 포괄하다 **subject** 주제; 과목 **sphere** 영역, 분야; 구 **attainment** 성취, 달성, 성과 **amount to** ~와 마찬가지이다, ~와 같다; (합계가) ~ 이다 **adap to** ~에 적응하다 **universal science** 보편적 과학 **proceed** 나아가다, 진행하다 **astonish** 깜짝 놀라게하다 **formula** 공식 **abbreviate** 축약하다 **sufficient** 충분한 **perception** 인식, 지각 **retain** 보유하다, 유지하다 **retention** 보유, 유지 **leave room for** ~을 위한 공간(여지)을 남겨두다 **regardless of** ~에 상관없이 **create space for** ~을 위한 공간을 만들다 **acquistion** 습득; 인수

5.

Suppose you just had a nasty fight with your boyfriend. The algorithm in charge of your sound system will immediately discern your inner emotional turmoil, and based on what it knows about you personally and about human psychology in general, it will play songs tailored to resonate with your gloom and echo your distress. These particular songs might not work well with other people but are just perfect for your personality type. After helping you get in touch with the depths of your sadness, the algorithm would then play the one song in the world that is likely to cheer you up – perhaps because your subconscious connects it with a happy childhood memory that even you are not aware of. No human DJ could ever hope to match the skills of such an AI.

— Adapted from Yuval Noah Harari, *21 Lessons for the 21st Century*, p. 35

in charge of ~을 책임지는, 담당하는 **discern** 식별하다 **turmoil** 혼란 **tailored** 맞춤화 된 **resonate** 울려 퍼지다, 반향하다 **gloom** 우울함 **echo** ~을 반영하다 **distress** 고통 **subconscious** 잠재의식

---

1. 위 글의 주제로 가장 알맞은 것은?

a. role of AI algorithm in shaping music preferences

b. effectiveness of AI algorithm in selecting personalized music

c. ability of AI algorithm to discern and address emotional distress through tailored music

d. limitations of human DJs in understanding individual emotional needs compared to AI

2. 주어진 단어를 사용하여 요지문을 완성하시오.

AI algorithm in a sound system can effectively _____

_____ by _____

_____ the skills of human DJs.

(an individual's emotional distress/ surpassing/ playing tailed songs/ discern and respond to)

요지: 사운드 시스템의 AI 알고리즘은 맞춤형 노래를 재생하여 개인의 정서적 고통을 효과적으로 식별하고 대응할 수 있으며, 인간 DJ 의 기술을 능가한다.

 *Explanations*

[해석]

방금 남자 친구와 심하게 싸웠다고 가정해 보자. 사운드 시스템을 담당하는 알고리즘은 내면의 감정적 혼란을 즉시 식별하고, 그리고 개인적으로 당신과 인간 심리 전반에 대해 알고 있는 것을 바탕으로 우울함을 달래고 당신의 고통을 반향 하도록 맞춤 화된 노래를 재생시킨다. 이 특정 노래들은 다른 사람들과 잘 어울리지 않을 수 있지만 당신의 성격 유형에는 완벽하다. 당신이 슬픔의 깊이와 접촉하는 것을 도와준 다음, 알고리즘은 당신을 격려할 수 있는 세상에서 하나 밖 게 없는 노래를 재생해 준다 – 아마도 당신의 잠재의식은 이 노래를 당신조차도 알지 못하는 행복한 어린 시절의 기억과 함께 연결시키기 때문일 것이다. 어떤 인간 DJ도 그러한 AI의 기술에 필적하기를 바랄 수 없다.

[해설]

1. 이 글의 주제로 **c**. The ability of AI algorithm to discern and address emotional distress through tailored music "맞춤형 음악을 통해 정서적 고통을 식별하고 해결해 주는 AI 알고리즘의 능력"이 가장 적절하다.

2. 이 글의 요지문은 다음과 같다:

AI algorithm in a sound system can effectively <u>discern and respond to an individual's emotional distress</u> by <u>playing tailored songs</u>, <u>surpassing</u> the skills of human DJs.

[어휘]

nasty 심한, 역겨운 **in charge of** ~을 책임지는, 담당하는 **discern** 식별하다 **turmoil** 혼란 **tailored** 맞춤화 된 **resonate** 울려 퍼지다, 반향하다 **gloom** 우울함 **echo** ~을 반영하다 **distress** 고통 **subconscious** 잠재의식 **be aware of** ~ 을 알다, 인지하다 **match** ~에 필적하다 **preference** 선호(도) **effectiveness** 유효성, 효과성 **personalized** 개인의 기호에 맞춰진 **address** 대처(해결)하다, 처리하다 **respond to** ~에 대응(응답, 반응)하다 **surpass** ~을 능가하다

Quote Break

《사피엔스》 (Sapiens: A Brief History of Humankind)의 저자인 유발 하라리(Yuval Harari)의 명언으로 "역사를 공부하는 이유"에 관한 글입니다.

"We study history *not* to know the future *but* to **widen** our **horizons**, to understand that our present situation is *neither* natural *nor* inevitable, and that we **consequently** have many more possibilities before us than we imagine."

"우리가 역사를 공부하는 것은 미래를 알기 위해서가 아니라 우리의 시야(지평)를 넓혀서 우리의 현재 상황이 당연한 것도 아니고 또한 필연적인 것도 아니다는 것을 이해하기 위한 것입니다. 또한 그에 따른 결과로 우리가 상상하는 것보다 더 많은 가능성이 우리 앞에 있다는 것을 이해하기 위해 우리는 역사를 공부합니다."

[어휘 & 표현]

not A but B: A가 아니라 B **widen** ~을 넓히다 **horizon** 시야, 지평 **neither A nor B**: A도 아니고 B도 아닌 **natural** 당연한, 자연적인 **inevitable** 필연적인, 피할 수 없는, 불가피한 **consequently** 결과적으로, 그에 따른 결과로

"History is something like a third **dimension** to human life. The first two dimensions are, of course, the present and the future, and it is their **interplay** that makes us what we are. But the third dimension—history—reminds us that what seems **obvious** or **natural** in the present is **not necessarily** so. Everything happens somewhere and at some time, and history is the map that **illuminates** these places and times, helping us understand ourselves and our world."

"역사는 인간의 삶에 대한 세 번째 차원과 같습니다. 물론 처음 두 차원은 현재와 미래이며, 우리를 현재의 우리로 만드는 것은 그들의 상호 작용입니다. 그러나 세 번째 차원인 역사는 우리에게 현재에는 명백하거나 자연스러워 보이는 것이 반드시 그런 것은 아니라는 것을 상기시켜줍니다. 모든 것은 어딘 가에서 그리고 어떤 시기에 일어납니다, 그리고 역사는 이러한 장소와 시간을 밝혀주는 지도이며, 그래서 우리 자신과 세상을 이해하는 데 도움을 줍니다."

[어휘 & 표현]

dimension 차원 **interplay** 상호작용 **obvious** 명백한 **natural** 당연한 **not necessarily** 반드시 ~ 인 것은 아닌 **illuminate** ~을 비추다, 밝히다, 규명하다

Answer Key

Chapter 1

1.1. What is a Topic?

PRACTICE 1

1. shape   2. position   3. car equipment   4. reference book   5. Planet
6. symptom   7. Currency   8. literature   9. household chores   10. environmental issues

PRACTICE 3

1. *Topic:* b. ways to calm down

2. *Topic:* a. ways to save money

3. *Topic:* b. importance of rainforest

4. *Topic:* c. development of clocks

5. *Topic:* b. practical jokes

PRACTICE 4

1. *Topic:* a. ways to enhance reading habits

2. *Topic:* a. ways to save money

3. *Topic:* a. impact of online streaming services

4. *Topic*: a. reasons why adolescents take drugs

1.2. What is a Paragraph?

Group A

[해석] 애완 동물의 세계에는 사람들이 동반자로 기르는 많은 종류의 동물이 있다. 개를 키우는 사람도 있고, 고양이를 키우는 사람도 있다. 물고기도 인기 있는 애완동물이다. 사람들은 애완 동물이 귀엽고 친교를 제공하기 때문에 애완 동물을 좋아한다. 개는 재주를 부리도록 훈련될 수 있고, 고양이는 안기는 것을 좋아한다. 물고기는 수조가 필요하며 규칙적으로 먹이를 주어야 한다. 반려동물을 돌보는 데는 많은 비용이 들고, 음식, 물, 관심을 주는 것도 까다롭다. 전반적으로, 반려동물을 가지는 것은 사람의 삶에 기쁨과 행복을 가져다 줄 수 있다.

[어휘] **companion** 동반자, 친구, 동료; 반려; (책) 안내서, 지침서 **companionship** 교제; 친교 **be trained** 훈련 받다 **do tricks** 묘기(재주)를 부리다 **cuddle** 안기다, ~을 포옹하다, 안다 **tank** 수조 **feed** ~에게 먹이를 주다 **cost** 비용이 들다 **demanding** 힘든, 까다로운 **overall** 전반적으로; 전반적인

Group B

[해석] 반려동물은 개인의 정서적 웰빙을 향상시키는 데 중요한 역할을 한다. 개나 고양이와 함께 있으면 편안함을 느끼고 외로움을 줄일 수 있다. 동물을 쓰다듬는 행위는 "유대감 호르몬(bonding hormone)"인 옥시토신을 분비하여 유대감과 행복감을 촉진한다. 연구에 따르면 반려동물과 상호 작용하면 스트레스 수준을 낮추고 전반적인 기분을 개선할 수 있다. 장난기 많은 새끼 고양이든 충직한 반려견이든 상관없이, 애완동물이 인간의 삶에 미치는 긍정적인 영향은 기쁨과 위안의 원천이다.

[어휘] **play a significant role in** ~에 상당한 역할을 하다 **enhance** 강화(향상)시키다 **companionship** 교제; 친교 **companion** 동반자, 친구, 동료; 반려; (책) 안내서, 지침서 **pet** (동물을) 애완 동물로 삼다; (남을) 귀여워하다(fondle), 쓰다듬다 **release** 방출하다, 분비하다 **promote** 촉진(장려)하다; 홍보하다 **a sense of connection** 유대감, 연대감 **lower** ~을 낮추다 **overall** 전반적인; 전반적으로 **loyal** 충성스러운, 충직한, 충실한 **canine** 개, 견, 강아지 **impact** 영향, (강한)충격 **source** 원(천), 근원

PRACTICE 1

Group 1

[해석] 사람들은 의학의 발전에 행복해한다. 그 후에 늘어난 출생 수에 대해서는 염려한다. 과학자들은 농 화학 분야에서 커다란 진보를 이루어, 식량 공급을 크게 증가시켰다. 그 후에 우리의 강은 너무 오염되어 수영조차 할 수 없다. 우리는 공중 수송의 발전에 행복해하고 거대한 비행기로 인해 감동받는다. 그 후에 비행기의 추락이나 공중전의 두려움에 놀라고 만다. 우리는 드디어 우주에 진입할 수 있다는 사실에 흥분한다. 그러나 우리는 의심할 여지없이 거기에서도 다른 또 한 면을 보게 될 것이다.

[해설] 과학 발전으로 이룩한 사실들의 장점과 아울러, 그것이 초래한 단점에 대해 각각 기술하고 있다. "과학 발전의 양면성"에 대한 글이다.

[어휘] **agricultural chemistry** 농 화학 **pollute** 오염시키다 **transportation** 운송 (기관) **impress** 감동시키다 **the other** 나머지 하나(의)

Group 2

[해석] 적은 관광객, 더 저렴한 가격, 더 아름다운 풍경을 원한다면 사그레스 반도(Sagres Peninsula)로 향하세요. 지역 박물관에는 의상, 무기 및 수공예품이 풍부하게 소장되어 있습니다. 버스를 타면 대부분의 장소로 갈 수 있지만 장거리 여행의 경우 기차가 더 저렴하고 편안합니다. 포르투갈 경제는 최근 몇 년 동안 매우 빠르게 확장되었지만 여전히 많은 문제를 안고 있습니다. 15 세기에 리스본(Lisbon)은 정치 권력과 종교와 문화의 세계적인 중심지였습니다.

[어휘] **scenery** 경치, 풍경 **head for** ~로 향하다 **peninsula** 반도 **collection** 소장, 모음집 **costume** 복장, 의상 **handicraft** 수공예품 **expand** 팽창하다 **rapidly** 급속하게 **religion** 종교

Group 3

[해석] 비디오 게임 세계에서 캐릭터 커스터마이징은 플레이어 참여를 향상시키는 필수 기능이 되었다. 플레이어는 게임 내 아바타의 외모, 기술 및 능력을 개별화하여 독특한 게임 경험을 만들 수 있다. 헤어스타일, 의상 또는 전문 기술을 선택하든 캐릭터 커스터마이징을 통해 플레이어는 자신의 개성을 표현하고 가상 세계에 몰입할 수 있다. 이 기능은 롤플레잉 게임의 인기 있는 측면이 되었으며, 이 게임에서 플레이어 캐릭터의 여정은 플레이어의 결정과 선호도에 따라 결정됩니다.

[어휘] **customization** 커스터마이징, (고객,사용자) 맞춤화, 주문형 **integral feature** 필수적인 기능(특징) **enhance** 강화(향상)시키다 **engagement** 참여, 몰입도; 약혼 **personalize** 개인화(개별화)하다 **outfit** (겉)옷, 복장, 차림새 **individuality** 개성 **immerse oneself in** ~에 몰입하다 **aspect** 측면 **preference** 선호, 선호도

Group 4

[해석] 인공 지능의 발전은 빠르게 진행되고 있다. 우리는 음성 인식 비서에서 자율 주행 자동차에 이르기까지 다양한 형태의 AI 를 보고 있다. AI 는 방대한 양의 데이터를 빠르게 분석할 수 있어 의료 및 금융과 같은 분야에 도움이 된다. 그러나 AI 가 어떻게 사용되는지에 대한 윤리적 우려가 있다. 일부는 개인 정보 보호 문제와 AI 의 잠재적 오용 가능성에 대해 우려한다. 다른 사람들은 AI 가 일자리 창출을 위한 새로운 길을 열어주어 데이터 분석, 머신 러닝, AI 개발에 기술을 갖춘 인력이 필요하다고 주장한다. 자동화와 AI 는 또한 기계가 이전에 인간이 수행했던 작업을 수행할 수 있게 됨에 따라 일자리 대체(이직)로 이어질 수 있다. 그래서 AI 기술의 발전을 수용함에 따라 이러한 윤리적 우려를 해결하는 것이 중요하다.

[어휘] **voice-activated assistant** 음성 인식 비서 **self-driving car** 자율 주행 자동차 **analyze** 분석하다 **finance** 금융 **ethical** 윤리적인 **potential misuse** 잠재적 오용 **open new avenues for** ~을 위한 새로운 길(장)을 열어주다 **workforce** 인력 **equipped with** ~로 장비를 갖춘, ~을 겸비한 **job displacement** 직업 이직(대체) **become capable of ~ing** ~할 수 있다 **crucial** 중대한, 중요한 **address** 해결하다 **embrace** 포용(수용)하다 **advancement** 진보, 발전

1.3. Topic of a Paragraph

PRACTICE 1

1. __T__ The dangers of smokers' blood

   __B__ The dangers of smoking

   __N__ How long pollutants stay in smokers' blood

2. __B__ Environmental problems

   __N__ Bathroom graffiti-makers

   __T__ Makers of graffiti

3. __B__ Fears

   __T__ Phobias

   __N__ Phobias about elevators

4.

   __T__ The superstition about the number thirteen.

   __N__ Buildings without a thirteenth floor

   __B__ Superstitions

5.

   __B__ Sleep

   __T__ Causes of sleepwalking

   __N__ The inherited tendency to sleepwalk

6.

   __N__ The privacy of celebrities

   __T__ The dark sides of fame

   __B__ The dangers of fame

7.

   __B__ Bad breath

   __T__ Causes of bad breath

   __N__ Bad breath caused by oral and throat infection

8.

   __B__ Computers on the job

   __T__ Tips for using a computer on the job

   __N__ Injuries caused by using a computer on the job

PRACTICE 1

1. 1) Garbage disposal   2) 1번재 문장
2. 1) Types of Discount Pricing   2) 1번째 문장
3. 1) c. Advantages of traditional classes   2) 2번째 문장
4. 1) b. The origin of potato chips   2) 1번째 문장

[해석 및 어휘 정리]

3.

[해석] 가상 학교가 언젠가는 전통적인 학교를 대체할 것인가? 문제점들이 있음에도 불구하고 전통적인 교실들은 온라인 교실보다 몇 가지 장점들이 있다. 무엇보다도, 전통적인 교실은 학생들이 서로서로 얼굴을 마주 대하면서 관계를 맺을 수 있는 장소이다. 다시 말하자면 컴퓨터의 자판이 악수의 따스함을 결코 대신할 수 없으며 또한 컴퓨터의 모니터가 다른 학생의 미소를 대신할 수도 없다. 전통적인 학교에서는, 학생들이 단체 운동, 동아리 활동, 그리고 학교축제에 참여할 수 있는데, 이런 것들은 컴퓨터를 통해서 배우는 학생들에게는 가능하지 않은 선택권이다.

[해설] 전통적인 학교가 첨단 가상 학교에 비해서 어떤 혜택을 더 누릴 수 있는지를 다루는 글이다.

[어휘] **replace** 대신하다, 대체하다 **in spite of** ~에도 불구하고 **hold** 잡다, 유지하다, 지니다 **advantage** 이점 **first of all** 무엇보다도, 우선 **relate** 관련시키다 **face to face** 직접적으로 **that is** 즉, 다시 말해서 **warmth** 따스함, 온기 **take part in** ~에 참여하다 **available** 이용할 수 **demand** 요구하다, 요구, 수요 **benefit** 이익, 이득, ~에게 이롭다 **origin** 기원, 원천, 근원 **limitation** 한계, 제한

1.4. What is the Main Idea

PRACTICE 2

Group 1

__MI__ a. The human skeleton has certain important functions.

__SD__ b. The skeleton gives the body support and shape.

__SD__ c. The skeleton protects internal organs.

__T__ d. The human skeleton.

Group 2

__MI__ a. TV has begun to deal with sex in a more realistic way.

__SD__ b. Couples on TV now openly discuss topics such as birth control.

__SD__ c. Bedroom scenes are now being shown in detail on some TV shows.

__T__ d. TV's treatment of sex.

Group 3

__SD__ a. One pitcher smooths the dirt on the pitcher's mound before he throws each pitch.

__SD__ b. One infielder sits in the same spot on the dugout bench during every game.

__MI__ c. Some baseball players think that certain superstitious habits help them win games.

__T__ d. Baseball players.

Group 4

__SD__ a. At dinnertime, instead of cooking many people simply go to a fast-food restaurant, or they send out for pizza or Chinese food.

__SD__ b. More and more families bring home prepared meals from the frozen-foods section of the "deli" counter.

__MI__ c. Home cooking is becoming a lost art.

__T__ d. Home cooking

Group 5

__SD__ a. Benjamin Franklin discovered that lightning is an electrical charge.

__MI__ b. In addition to being a statesman, Franklin was a scientist and an inventor.

__T__ c. Benjamin Franklin's work.

__SD__ d. Franklin invented bifocals, the Franklin stove, and an electric storage battery.

Group 6

__SD__ a. Scientists used to think of the brain as the center of an electrical communication system.

__MI__ b. The way scientists view the brain's role has changed greatly.

__SD__ c. Today it is known that "the brain is a bag of hormones," as one scientist puts it.

__T__ d. How scientists think about the role of the brain.

Group 7

__SD__ a. Adults seek out spicy or bitter foods to stimulate their smaller supply of taste buds.

__T__ b. Sensitivity to flavors.

__MI__ c. The difference in the sensitivity to flavors between children and adults lies in the taste buds, the tiny taste receptors that line the tongue.

__SD__ d. Young children's tongues are loaded with taste buds and are especially sensitive; therefore, sour or spicy flavors seem too intense to them.

Group 8

MI a. Procrastination has two possible causes.

SD b. Many people may procrastinate because they have a fear of failure, and if they don't begin a task or project, they can't fail at it.

T c. Causes of procrastination

SD d. Others may procrastinate out of laziness; these careless workers have not yet developed a strong work ethic.

Group 9

MI a. A snake can control its body temperature in two ways.

SD b. First, a snake can darken its skin to absorb higher levels of solar heat; once its body reaches a suitable temperature, the snake can lighten its skin color.

SD c. A snake also spreads and flattens its body as it lies at a right angle to the sun's rays to expose more of its body and raise its temperature; to reduce its body temperature, a snake lies parallel to the sun's rays or moves into the shade.

T d. Ways a snake controls its body temperature

PRACTICE 3

Group 1

__MI__ a. The Covid-19 pandemic significantly affected education worldwide, bringing about new and difficult changes.

__T__ b. The impact of the Covid-19 pandemic on education.

__SD__ c. Remote learning technologies have become essential tools in the face of pandemic-related closures.

__SD__ d. The pandemic also made it clear that not all students had equal access to technology and the internet, which made it harder for some to keep learning.

__SD__ e. The pandemic prompted educators to innovate, adopting virtual classrooms, online assessments, and collaborative platforms.

Group 2

__SD__ a. Disagreeing parties can accept the *status quo*, agreeing to just live with the situation as it stands.

__MI__ b. When faced with a disagreement, the parties involved have several ways to proceed.

__SD__ c. One party may use physical, social, or economic force to impose a solution on the others.

__SD__ d. Negotiation, or reaching a mutually acceptable solution, is a means of dealing with conflict.

__T__ e. Various ways for the parties to proceed in case of disagreement.

Group 3

__MI__ a. Algorithms play a significant role in curating and recommending online content.

__SD__ b. By analyzing user preferences, behavior, and data, algorithms can personalize the online experience by suggesting articles, videos, and ads that are likely to be of interest to individuals.

__SD__ c. There are concerns about the potential biases and echo chambers that algorithms may create, as they can reinforce existing beliefs and limit exposure to diverse perspectives.

__SD__ d. Algorithms are employed to filter user-generated content on platforms, removing content that violates community guidelines to maintain a safe and respectful online environment.

__T__ e. The role of algorithms in shaping online content.

Group 4

__SD__ a. K-pop music groups like BTS and BLACKPINK have gained immense popularity, breaking records and topping charts not only in South Korea but also internationally.

__SD__ b. Korean dramas, known for their unique storytelling and high production quality, have attracted a global audience, leading to remakes and adaptations in various countries.

__MI__ c. The Korean Wave, also known as Hallyu, has made a significant impact on popular culture worldwide.

__SD__ d. The influence of Korean fashion and beauty trends can be seen in the global market, with K-beauty products gaining popularity and Korean fashion brands becoming sought-after worldwide.

__T__ e. The global impact of the Korean Wave

Training 적용 훈련 문제

1.

1) 주제문의 위치? __1__

2) 글의 주제로 가장 적절한 것은? b. Increase in the number of endangered and threatened species

2.

1) 주제문의 위치? __2__

2) 글의 주제로 가장 적절한 것은? b. Studies on the impact of pet ownership on well-being

3.

1) 주제문의 위치? __2__

2) 글의 주제로 가장 적절한 것은? b. The living conditions of naimals in zoos

4.

1) 주제문 2개의 위치는? __1, 7__

2) 글의 주제로 가장 적절한 것은? a. Efficiency of photo radar in traffic law enforcement

Chapter 2

PRACTICE 1

1.

1) 주제문의 위치? __3__

2) 글의 주제로 가장 적절한 것은? c. Inflence of physical attractiveness on personal perceptions

2.

1) 주제문의 위치? __1__

2) 글의 주제로 가장 적절한 것은? b. The strenth of spider silk compared to steel

3.

1) 주제문의 위치? __4__

2) 글의 주제로 가장 적절한 것은? b. Need for professional treatment for eating disorders

4.

1) 주제문의 위치? __7__

2) 글의 주제로 가장 적절한 것은? a. Challenge of differenciating hot and cold through touch

5.

1) 주제문의 위치? __5__

2) 글의 주제로 가장 적절한 것은? b. Cultural variations in teaching self-perception

6.

1) 주제문 2개의 위치는? __1, 9__

2) 글의 주제로 가장 적절한 것은? a. Challenges faced by judges in staying awak during trials

7.

1) 주제문 2개의 위치는? __1, 9__

2) 글의 주제로 가장 적절한 것은? d. Persistence and determination in the history of inventors

4. [해석] Hot and cold는 우리가 온도를 어떻게 인지하는지 설명하기 위해 사용하는 주요한 두 단어이다. 이 두 단어는 매우 어린 나이에 우리의 의식에 각인되어 있다. 그리고 대부분 우리는 그 둘의 차이를 구별하는 데 문제가 없다. 그러나 때때로 그 차이는 완전히 명확하지 않다. 예를 들어, 만약 당신이 눈을 가리고 있었고 누군가가 먼저 뜨거운 다리미로 당신을 터치한 다음 드라이아이스 조각으로 당신을 터치하면, 당신은 아마도 뜨거운 것과 차가운 것을 구별할 수 없을 것이다. 이것은 주요 사실을 보여주는 단순한 증거이다. <u>생리학적 또는 신체적 반응은 온도를 측정하는 신뢰할 수 있는 방법이 아니다.</u>

5. [해석] 미국, 호주, 그리고 서유럽에서 사람들은 독립적이 되도록 권장된다. 이 문화권의 구성원들은 앞서가고, 경쟁하고, 이기고, 목표를 성취하고, 자신의 고유한 잠재력을 실현하도록, 군중으로부터 눈에 띄도록 교육을 받는다. 많은 아시아와 아프리카 국가에서, 사람들은 상호 의존적인 자아에 가치를 두도록 배운다. 이 문화권의 구성원들은 사이좋게 지내고, 다른 사람들을 돕고, 그리고 의견에 맞서거나 눈에 띄지 않도록 교육을 받는다. <u>따라서, 사람들이 어떤 식으로 그들 자신을 바라보도록 교육받는 방식에는 상당한 문화적 차이가 있다.</u>

Chapter 3

3.2. Step-by-Step Guide

STEP 1. 암시된 포괄적 내용(Implied General Idea) 찾기

1. *General idea is:* c. *major life events.*

2. *General idea is:* c. inventions for seeing.

3. *General idea is:* c. complaints.

4. *General idea is:* c. explanations for being late.

STEP 2. 암시된 포괄적 내용(Implied General Idea) 직접 쓰기

1. General idea: Parts of a <u>book</u>

2. General idea: ways of <u>cooking eggs</u>

3. General idea: Jobs in a <u>restaurant</u>

4. General idea: things that are white

5. General idea: ways to <u>get a good grade in school</u>

STEP 3. 암시된 요지(Implied Main Idea) 찾기

PRACTICE 1

Group 1: d. Lasers are used in a variety of ways.

Group 2: b. Various factors can contribute to heart disease.

Group 3: b. An octopus has several means of defense.

Group 4: b. Pyramids are massive structures, whose contents reflect the ancient Egyptians' beliefs.

STEP 4. 문단내에 암시된 요지(Implied Main Idea) 찾기

PRACTICE 2

1. c. The fear of crossing the path of a black cat comes from beliefs about witches in the Middle Ages.

2. a. Two office workers learned that birds could get drunk.

3. b. Before much was known about germs, doctors unknowingly cause much illness and death by spreading germs.

4. c. The history of frozen desserts was influenced by Nero and Marco Polo.

5. a. Eating a good breakfast increases one's efficiency throughout the day.

STEP 5. 암시된 요지(Implied Main Idea)를 직접 쓰기

Training 적용 훈련 문제

1.
   1) **Topic:** <u>bad dream or frightening dream</u>

   2) **Implied main idea:** I <u>had a really frightening dream</u>.

2.
   1) **Topic:** <u>A survey of patients</u>

   2) **The implied main idea:** A survey of patients shows that <u>serious illness can have positive effects after their illness</u>.

   3) **Paraphrasing:** A survey of patients shows that many individuals <u>who have suffered serious illnesses experience positive changes</u> in their lives.

3.
   1) **Topic:** <u>Children's toy preference</u>

   2) **Implied main idea:** At different development stages, children like specific kinds of toys.

   3) **Paraphrasing:** Children's toy <u>preferences</u> are <u>influenced by their developmental stages</u>.

4.
   1) **Topic:** <u>curing hiccups</u>

   2) **Implied main idea:** There are <u>some odd remedies</u> for <u>curing hiccups</u>.

   3) **Paraphrasing:** Various <u>unconventional methods</u> are suggested as <u>potential cures for hiccups</u>.

5.
   1) **Topic:** Eclipses

   2) **Implied main idea:** Eclipses are <u>culturally significant</u> to many <u>societies</u>.

   3) **Paraphrasing:** Eclipses are <u>culturally significant</u> and have <u>varied interpretation</u> across <u>different societies and civilizations</u>.

6.

   1) Topic: <u>common medical beliefs</u>

   2) Implied main idea: Many <u>common medical beliefs</u> are <u>misconceptions or falsehoods</u>.

   3) Paraphrasing: <u>Common medical beliefs</u>, such as chocolate causing pimples, sucking snakebites to prevent poisoning, and drinking milk for ulcers, <u>are false</u>.

7.

   1) Topic: <u>dietary guidelines</u>

   2) Implied main idea: Certain <u>dietary guidelines</u> can help you <u>recover from an illness</u>.

   3) Paraphrasing: Certain dietary guidelines can be <u>beneficial</u> in <u>promoting recovery</u> and <u>minimizing discomfort</u> during illness.

결국은 문해력 시리즈의 '**제1권 주제·요지편**'은 단순히 문장 해석을 넘어서 문장과 문장과의 논리적 전개와 한글과 다른 영어의 글 전개 구조를 이해하도록 도와줄 것입니다. 그리고 독해의 핵심 능력인 주제와 요지 그리고 뒷받침 글을 파악하고 암시된 요지를 추론하는데 필요한 논리적인 사고를 향상시키는 데에 중점을 두고 있습니다.

"결국은 문해력" 시리즈는 총 7 권으로 구성될 예정입니다. 향후 출시될 "결국은 문해력" 시리즈는 제 2 권 핵심과 뒷받침 글 구별하기, 제 3 권 글 전개방식 익히기, 제 4 권 글 순서와 문장 넣기, 제 5 권 요약과 패러프레이징, 제 6 권 추론하기, 제 7 권 Fact Vs Opinion 등 입니다. 각 권마다 영어 독해력과 문해력을 높이기 위한 다양한 전략과 실전 연습이 계속해서 제시되며 수업생들의 영어 실력이 한 단계씩 발전되기를 기대합니다.

제1권
주제·요지

제7권
Fact vs
Opinion

제2권
핵심과
뒷받침 글

결국은
문해력
시리즈

제3권
전개방식
익히기

제6권
추론하기

제5권
요약과
패러프레이징

제4권
글 순서와
문장 넣기

이성태
현, TED 영어 원장
현, 육군 3 사관학교 토익강사
토익 만점 강사
수능,토익,토플,텝스 17 년 강의 경력
북미(미국,캐나다) 6 년 거주
University of British Columbia ESL
경북대 대학원 영문학 석사
경북대 대학원 영문학 박사과정